Breaking free from the Poverty Mentality

Michele Michaels

Foreword by
Erin Thiele

RestoreMinistries.net

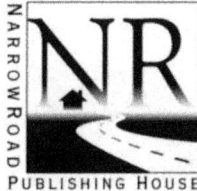

NarrowRoad Publishing House

Michele Michaels
Breaking free from the Poverty Mentality

Published by:
NarrowRoad Publishing House
POB 830
Ozark, MO 65721 U.S.A.

The materials from Restore Ministries were written for the sole purpose of encouraging women. For more information, visit us at:

EncouragingWomen.org
RestoreMinistries.net

Unless otherwise indicated, most Scripture verses are taken from the *New American Standard Bible* (NASB). Scripture quotations marked KJV are taken from the *King James Version* of the Bible, and Scripture quotations marked NIV are taken from the *New International Version*. Our ministry is not partial to any particular version of the Bible but **loves** them all so that we are able to help every woman in any denomination who needs encouragement and who has a desire to gain greater intimacy with her Savior.

Cover Design by Tara Thiele

ISBN: 1-931800-17-0
ISBN13: 978-1-931800-17-4
Library of Congress Control Number: 2019905341

Contents

Foreword

It's both exciting and rewarding to see this book finally becoming a reality. Michele and I have had a long lovely friendship for years soon after she helped me with editing and proofing our RMI books. Our working relationship developed into a true admiration for Michele, which now has led to the honor of writing the forward to her first Real Life Novel.

You'll notice that we have given Michele permission to use portions of other RMI books and also testimonies submitted and sent to RMI. These confirm what Michele is saying that I'm certain will both motivate and encourage you to seek God for wisdom as she has done and also to make the Lord your most prized and cherished relationship as she exhibits throughout this amazing book.

Don't read this book just once, make sure it's your go to when facing any litigation to stay moving along that narrow path that leads to live—the abundant life He died to give us.

Erin Thiele
Restore Ministries International

———————— Chapter 1 ————————

The Poverty Mentality Defined

"And my God **will** supply all your needs
according to His riches..."
— Philippians 4:19

So many women, especially women who are the sole providers of
their household, seem to fall into what I have begun referring to as
the "Poverty Mentality." The Poverty Mentality is when we use
phrases such as, "I can't afford it" or "I'm on a tight budget" and any
other way we slander or shame our heavenly Husband. The danger
is, as these phrases and mindset become a part of your vocabulary, it
very soon gets buried, entering your heart, and the enemy steals your
peace from you.

"For the mouth speaks out of that which fills the heart" (Matthew
12:34).

It's very easy to slip into this mindset and mental stronghold,
especially when it's **you who** pays the bills or begins to take over the
finances after a divorce. It can hit when you read your divorce
papers, what it says you are going to get in the settlement, like the
first time I foolishly read through my divorce papers. Or like me this
time, when you total up your family's debt, where you'd been hoping
to consolidate the debt you believed was there in order to qualify for

a lower percentage loan, but find the amount of debt your ex-husband has left you is hundreds of times larger.

Make no mistake, this sort of thinking and how we speak is a clear and deliberate trap from the enemy—primarily because it is contrary to what Scripture says, and who our Father is, who our Husband is. No, I am not trying to be "spiritually weird" here and encourage us to all go out and buy whatever we want because our spiritual "Sugar Daddy" will pay for it! But let's each be very careful that we don't fall into thinking like the world, speaking like the world and therefore worrying like the world does—wondering about *how* **we** will make it financially—when the Bible *promises* that God will take care of **all** not just **some** of our needs, but based on His riches!

"And my God will supply **all your needs** according to His riches in glory in Christ Jesus" (Philippians 4:19).

Amplified: "And my God will liberally supply (fill until full) your every need according to His riches in glory in Christ Jesus."

Living Bible: "And it is He who will supply all your needs from his riches in glory because of what Christ Jesus has done for us."

Message: "You can be sure that God will take care of everything you need, his generosity exceeding even yours in the glory that pours from Jesus."

If you and I can believe that what Jesus did for us is enough to cover our salvation, and maybe a few other areas of our life, then why not believe Him for everything, including our financial needs, wants, and even our desires because it says that He *longs* to give them to us? Do you believe that He only covered most of your sins, but not all of them? Then how could He possibly not provide all you need financially, especially when He also says,

"Therefore the LORD **longs to be gracious** to you, and therefore He waits on high to have compassion on you. For the LORD is a God of justice; how blessed are all those who long for Him" (Isaiah 30:18).

In addition to your own peace of mind and well-being, there's another reason why we must shift our trust entirely to Him, because God says that without faith it is impossible to please Him (Hebrews 11:6). So, if we look at our finances without faith and blurt out to everyone, "We can't afford it" or "I don't know how we are going to make it" or "I'm on a tight or limited budget" or even saying "I have to watch my budget," it is like a slap in the face to our heavenly Father and it grieves our Husband reflecting how poor of a Man He is. God never says you need to budget the amount of sin Jesus' blood can cover, nor that He has limited resources to cover you financially. Let's look at this in another way.

How would you feel if your son or daughter told people, like their friends or their teachers at school, that they didn't know if they would be able to "afford" to eat lunch that day; maybe because they were on a budget, when they never asked you for lunch money, or they did but didn't trust you'd provide enough for the next week, so they decided they couldn't afford to trust you?

What if your children walked around the mall with torn up shoes, and when someone stopped to stare, they said they were on a "budget" so they weren't sure if they'd be able to afford to buy the new shoes that they needed? How would you feel if your children shamed you like that? And what would their friends (or people they met) think of you as a parent? Wouldn't they be outraged that you should be able to at least provide for your child's needs, especially if your children had been telling everyone that you were rich and generous? Of course!

It's exactly the same as when you shame your heavenly Father. When you tell people you're a believer, a child of God, yet then you continue to slander His good name and shame Him by telling people that, though you *are* a child of God (again that you profess to everyone), He is unable or unwilling to provide you with what you need, that you can barely make it, and you don't know where you will get enough money to pay your bills. This has to be a painful slap in the face to the One whom we profess to love and trust, and who owns everything here on earth—whose resources are endless.

Okay, so maybe you don't go around telling everyone, you just keep it to yourself, but your appearance shouts the same message to everyone. Your clothes are old and you haven't bought anything new in years, you let the roots grow out in your hair and you don't keep your hair cut in a current style. And your reason for not looking your best is because you *see* that if you take care of any of your own needs, you're sure you won't have enough money for shoes for your children or you're sure you won't be able to pay your bills. The sad truth is, you're the picture of poverty, even though you have a heavenly Father who has all that you need. A Husband who longs to treat you as His bride.

"Now faith is the assurance of things hoped for, the conviction of things **not seen**" (Hebrews 11:1).

In order to break free from the poverty mentality, you need to begin taking care of what He's already given you: your appearance, your home, your lawn, your car (inside and out), and also your children— since each reflects Who *has* faithfully taken care of you. Then whenever you have anything you need, or even something you want, just simply ask your Father or your Husband for it—He is just waiting for you to ask! Trust me, He wants to bless you with good things, just so long as you take care of what He has entrusted to you, and you show your gratitude by what comes out of your mouth; what you say to others, and by how you live.

Gratitude is all He asks in return; simply praising Him to others, sharing how awesomely giving your Father is, letting them know how lovingly generous your Husband is—so that people you know or meet will also want a relationship with the One Whom you admire and trust! It's very important that you never forget Who it is who *gave* the blessings to you either, because it says, "… you may say in your heart, 'My power and the strength of my hand made me this wealth.' But you shall remember the LORD your God, for it is **He** who **is giving you power to make wealth**, that He may confirm His covenant which He swore to your fathers, as it is this day" (Deuteronomy 8:17–18). The world believes you need a good education, a good paying job or some earthly inheritance to live abundantly—but that's only because they're attempting to do everything on their own—independent from the One who longs to care for and love them.

Sadly, when a Christian believes they are poor, their countenance, appearance, and what they **say** and do always reflects poverty. Yet, if a person believes they are rich (according to His riches in Christ Jesus) then their countenance, appearance, and everything that they say and do will radiate wealth!

Financial Testimony #1

"My Husband is Rich!

While Erin was visiting me, she told me a story I'd read about before, but hadn't heard directly from her until then. So, it's with her permission that I share it here:

My husband used to get irritated with me because I always told everyone that we were "rich!" Saying I was rich all began years ago when I saw a very poor tall black man who was trying to sell some pecans in a fast food hamburger restaurant in order to buy something to eat. When they said no to him at the counter, I went up and asked if I could buy him a meal. He said, "No, that's okay" after looking at me, then looking down at the floor. Without thinking, I said, "Well, my husband is very rich and he would want me to buy you something to eat." So, I paid for his meal and went back to my table. What I said was not a lie; in comparison to what this man had—even my earthly husband was very rich!

Later, when the man got his tray of food, he walked up and asked if he could sit with me. I could smell that he reeked of alcohol and filth, but I said, "Please do." Without looking up, keeping his eyes on his food, he asked me, "Why did you do that? Why did you buy me this food?" I told him that God had sent me there because he was hungry, and God just wanted him to know that He loved him. I said that I was on my way to church for the Revival that night and really wasn't even hungry because I'd had dinner, but I sensed I needed to come in and sit to wait since God had sent me. Then I told him when I heard him trying to sell the pecans for some food, I knew why God had sent me there that night—God loved him and He wanted him to know that He cared for him very much.

The man took another bite then asked me about the revival he'd seen going on, and when I was done and he was done eating, he said, "I'll go to church with you." I replied, "But there are no strings attached to me buying your meal. You don't need to go anywhere or do anything. He simply loves you." His reply was, "If you're willing to take me, I want to go." As we walked out, it was then that I realized everyone in the restaurant hadn't been talking, but instead had been listening to our entire conversation.

As we walked out to my van and he got in, I saw every eye was still on us, including the staff of the restaurant, many of whom had come out from the kitchen to witness what was going on. Since we were late (this being a huge, worldwide revival in Pensacola, Florida going on late in the 1990s when people would get in line before sunrise just to get in), I knew there wouldn't be any parking available (possibly forcing us to walk several blocks), but as I turned the corner suddenly I noticed a parking spot right by the front door (God had gone before us).

When I walked through the doors with this heavily soiled black man you would have thought I had entered with a king! The ushers came over and gave him a royal welcome, put their arms around him and opened the main door, and as they did a couple were walking out and said they were leaving, so the usher walked him down the aisle and seated him just a few rows from the front of the church. I turned and headed up to the balcony, finding a space along the side where I could stand to watch. At the end of the service this man was the first at the altar. I saw him on his knees weeping, and that evening he was transformed after accepting His love that changes lives.

A minute later I felt a hand on my shoulder, and when I turned, I saw it was the senior usher who sat me down to "reprimand" me, warning me about my foolishness and the danger I'd put myself in by driving this man to the Revival. Later when I got home, my husband and sons also made me promise I would never do anything like that again. Though I was disappointed that everyone failed to see this was a decision that changed the course of eternity for one soul, I knew in my heart that something amazing had happened, something that was all due to having experienced His love, knowing and hearing His voice, and being in a position to be used to share His love with someone so worthy. Knowing we were rich, God called me to play a very small part in witnessing His power and love to save that man's soul, where he finally experienced His love and His peace.

The point in Erin's testimony is this: Our finances and wealth are not so we can store up riches on earth, but so that we can be used by God (in big and small ways) to advance His kingdom. Whatever the man's meal cost or the danger she'd put herself in is really nothing in comparison to the reward she was able to witness. But, unless you are faithful in small things, you have the relationship with the Lord that enables you to hear and follow His lead, and you are willing to invest whatever you have, even and especially if you're lacking in anything right now, then you will never be given significant wealth that He wants to entrust you with in order to help bless others!

"And the one also who had received the one talent came up and said, 'Master, I knew you to be a hard man, reaping where you did not sow and gathering where you scattered no seed.

And I was afraid, and went away and hid your talent in the ground. See, you have what is yours.' But his master answered and said to him, 'you wicked, lazy slave, you knew that I reap where I did not sow and gather where I scattered no seed.

Then you ought to have put my money in the bank, and on my arrival I would have received my money back with interest. Therefore take away the talent from him, and give it to the one who has the ten talents. For to everyone who has, more shall be given, and he will have an abundance; but from the one who does not have, even what he does have shall be taken away" (Matthew 25:24–29).

Chapter 2

What Do You Believe?

"You say you have faith,
for you believe that there is one God.
Good for you!
Even the demons believe this,
and they tremble in terror."
—James 2:19 NLT

Most Christians can quote very few verses from the Bible. Most can recite John 3:16 and a few, I believe, also could quote our opening verse from Chapter 1, Philippians 4:19 *"And my God will supply all your needs **according to His riches** in Christ Jesus."* Nevertheless, just because we know this verse and may be able to quote it word for word, may I ask: How many of you *really believe* what this verse actually says? We may *say* we believe it, and quote it, but does our life reflect this belief?

Day in and day out we fight **doubt** and experience **lack** that are destined to rob our minds, hearts, and our confidence. Rather than living in the abundance of His riches, we struggle. This book is not just about our financial needs being met, though it will take up a good portion of it, but much more—it is about living this verse "my God will supply all your needs" in every area of our lives, and to reflect upon the greatest need He gave us—our heavenly Husband and His love.

This means, if we are indeed daughters of a Father who is the Creator of the universe, who states boldly, "'The silver is Mine and the gold is Mine,' declares the LORD of hosts" (Haggai 2:8) and "For every beast of the forest is Mine, the cattle on a thousand hills. I know every bird of the mountains, and everything that moves in the field is Mine" (Psalm 50:10-11), then it means we should never lack anything—nothing at all.

The apostles experienced this incredible phenomenon themselves, and just to remind them of God's ability to provide supernaturally, Jesus "said to them, 'When I sent you out without money belt and bag and sandals, you did not lack anything, did you?' They said, 'No, nothing'" (Luke 22:35).

Yet even knowing this truth, and no matter how many times God "shows up" by providing not just all we *need*, but very often most of what we *want*, we still speak or act and react as though we were impoverished orphans! How often have you caught yourself telling someone, even your children, "We (or I) can't afford it" or you make sure you make it clear to others about some sort of "budget" when the Bible encourages the opposite mindset?

To compound our fate, our lack of giving also reflects what we believe and is an intricate part of the missing puzzle piece keeping us from living abundantly, contributing to our foolishness, when we wrongly act like God asks us to give to Him because He needs our money. The truth is, the only reason He asks us to give to Him or to others is so that we can experience the JOY when we see the fruits of sowing into what He is doing here on earth. So He set up a system, it's called a tithe (which actually translates to 10%), so that our hearts will be intricately tied to His work. "For where your **treasure** is there will be your **heart** also" (Matthew 6:21). For those who begin to tithe, He then nudges them onto *real* giving, when we give beyond our means and present our offerings to Him.

Another myth that we must rise above is that we are only expected to give to God or to others out of our "abundance," when He actually tells us that our faith "is being sure of what we hope for and certain of what we *do not* see" (Hebrews 11:1 NIV). Read how the Message Bible explains this verse where true faith must be entirely unseen. "The fundamental fact of existence is that this trust in God, this faith, is the firm foundation under everything that makes life worth living. It's our handle on what we *can't see.* The act of faith is what distinguished our ancestors, set them above the crowd." I agree. This kind of faith is what makes life worth living.

Do you know what really gets God's attention? It's when we give to Him (and others) when we are in need or lack—this goes for being in need financially and in every other area of our life (like giving our time when we have none to give or giving encouragement when we need encouragement ourselves). Who can forget what Jesus said about the widow who gave the last she had in Mark 12:41-44 "Jesus sat down opposite the treasury, where people came to bring their offerings, and He watched as they came and went. Many rich people threw in large sums of money, but a poor widow came and put in only two small coins worth only a fraction of a cent."

"Jesus (calling His disciples together): Truly this widow has given a greater gift than any other contribution. All the others gave a little out of their great abundance, but this poor woman has given God everything she has" (The Voice).

What good is being a child of God, set apart from everyone in the world (who have yet to know Him), if we act, respond, and look at our needs as unmet or something that has to be "earned" or "worked for" or "begged and pleaded for" when it says clearly in Scripture: "It is vain for you to rise up early, to retire late, to eat the bread of painful labors; for He *gives* to His beloved even in his sleep" (Psalm 127:2)? And also in Deuteronomy 8:18 when it says, "But you shall remember the LORD your God, for it is **He** who is *giving* you **power**

to make wealth, that He may confirm His covenant which He swore to your fathers, as it is this day."

Yet, oh how easily those horrid words roll from our tongue "I can't afford it" and how accepted this concept is, even for a believer, especially for those of us who are single parents. I know.

May I be totally honest with you? This entire "poverty mentality" became one of my biggest hurdles to overcome. The battle began the day that the divorce agreement, which my husband filed, and that I had agreed to, became law, which meant that I legally (or officially) became responsible for an unimaginable mound of debt I'd known nothing about. And along with the debt, I'd also agreed to receiving no child support for any of my children who were living at home when my ministry and book sales (our sole income) was collapsing. To add to it, God saw fit to send my niece to live with us for a year, and a month later, He asked me to take care of my special needs sister, becoming her caregiver.

Was God trying to bury me? Or, was He in fact, once again, stacking the odds against me in order that I would be forced to totally rely on Him, and so that He alone would be glorified? Why did God put the story of Gideon in the Bible if not for us to see that if He saw fit to reduce the army he had to defend them from 32,000 men to just 300 men, that God, on purpose, wanted to prove just Whose power it is.

"The LORD said to Gideon, 'The people who are with you are too many for Me to give Midian into their hands, for Israel would become boastful, saying, 'My own power has delivered me'" (Judges 7:2).

Let's be honest, we're all alike; unless God creates a situation whereby there is no way out and we can't help ourselves—we will take all the credit. "Otherwise, you may say in your heart, 'My power and the strength of my hand made me this wealth'" (Deuteronomy 8:17). Being a "single parent" of a houseful of children and having others depending on me was just God's way of stacking the odds—

in order that He could supernaturally bless me (my family and my ministry).

Surprisingly for many, especially my ex-husband who more than once told me angrily that I was "going to lose the house" due to my continued giving, I am still living in and regularly have been making improvements on it. I believe that I hear the Lord who "sits in the heavens laughs, the Lord scoffs at them" (Psalms 2:4) who believe that divorce inevitably will destroy us—and that a big family equals poverty. Not so.

It is only when we forget Who our Father and Provider is. "And my God will supply all your needs **according to *His riches*** in glory in Christ Jesus" (Philippians 4:19). The Message "And now I have it all—and keep getting more! The gifts you sent... You can be sure that God will take care of everything you need, His generosity exceeding even yours in the glory that pours from Jesus. Our God and Father abounds in glory that just pours out into eternity. Yes."

It is only when we forget who our true Husband is (for each of us who have been rejected and forsaken) that fear and doubt takes over, which He begins by saying: "Fear not, for you will not be put to shame; and do not feel humiliated, for you will not be disgraced; but you will forget the shame of your youth, and the reproach of your widowhood you will remember no more."

"For your Husband is your Maker, Whose name is the LORD of hosts; and your Redeemer is the Holy One of Israel, Who is called the God of all the earth. For the LORD has called you, like a wife forsaken and grieved in spirit, even like a wife of one's youth when she is rejected,' Says your God" (Isaiah 54:4–6).

It's only when we forget Who we belong to, who our Father is, when we will fall prey to the poverty mentality and its downward spiral into true financial poverty. Though things do appear hopeless and terrifying, God always writes the last chapter "so that from the rising of the sun to the place of its setting men may know there is none besides me. I am the LORD, and there is no other. I form the light and create darkness, I bring prosperity and create disaster; I, the LORD, do all these things" (Isaiah 45:6–7 NIV).

Now, before rushing onto the next chapter, please take a moment, or better yet, a day or even a full week to think about the promises that we say we believe, but fail to live.

Once we live what we say we believe, others will soon witness that our entire existence is entirely to reflect the goodness of a Father who provides for ALL of our needs since He is so rich and full of glory! God our Father, Who provided His Son to care for and love us abundantly.

Financial Testimony #2

"You Never Asked"

Though I cannot tell you how many times I have shared this testimony and principle with family, friends, and even strangers, each time I do I believe I am just as blessed and encouraged as they have been, I could not write a book about finances without putting it in print.

As I've said, my journey of trusting God *totally* with my finances really began when my husband filed for divorce a second time. Prior to that, I had total and complete faith in trusting the Lord for our family and ministry, and it was my husband who had handled all our finances throughout our marriage. And over the course of all those years, there had to have been a dozen or more times when my husband would tell me that my faith in Him providing was only due to the fact that I did not handle the finances. I honestly thought he exaggerated the truth, but now I know that it IS a much harder walk of faith when it is *you* who is responsible because you can *see* how bleak your finances actually look.

When that fateful day arrived, my husband, while leaving for his appointment with the attorney, announced clearly that he would never pay any child support (he hadn't paid anything the first time he'd left us) and that he was leaving all (not just some) of our debt to me. Once the divorce was filed, he told me he was done, and from then on I was on my own.

Then, one day while doing the laundry, I began daydreaming about those beautiful front load washers that say they hold 17 pairs of jeans. I couldn't help it, I told the Lord how nice it would be to have a beautiful large front load washer since I had been doing the laundry for our large family and the loads had only increased since my husband leaving. That's when the Lord spoke to me and said, "But you never asked me Michele." So, with a heart bursting with faith, I blurted out enthusiastically, "Well, then I am asking you now. Lord, I would absolutely LOVE a front load large capacity washer and dryer!!"

Immediately, the moment I clicked on the switch and started the washer, it made the most horrible sound—yet I was ecstatic—I just knew it meant I was going to get my front loads!! Yippee!!!

My ex-husband, however, stormed in and said sternly, (after the children told him) shouting, "Are you serious Michele?! It only means, that you need a repairman!" When he said that, I didn't reply as he stormed out. Instead I just stood there, stunned, thinking to myself, "I can only imagine what it must have been like to be married to a wife like me. But I can't help myself, all I know to do is take everything that God says as gospel truth and when anyone believes with a "childlike faith" it has to be frustrating for everyone around you if they don't believe."

Even though I felt horrible at the wife I'd been to my ex, and another reason why he'd probably left me, very soon after while doing the laundry again, the Lord whispered, reminding me of what He'd promised, and told me to act on it: that I was to go to the store and purchase them. When I got to the store I immediately found out that there was a huge sale going on, with 24 no-interest payments. Incredible. The salesman wrote everything up, but I backed out. I suddenly felt horribly foolish for doing something so irresponsible.

My ex-husband was right, he'd told me countless times (and told my children too) that because of the way I handled finances (due primarily to the testimony I will share in the next chapter), we would soon lose everything, including our home. That day while looking at the front load washer and dryer, those words settled deep within my heart as I walked out without buying them.

The very next week I was on a plane to Colorado for my very first ministry trip. While there I got a call from my secretary who told me that a member of my fellowship, who I'd been ministering to via email just emailed and was sending in ten thousand dollars from Singapore! After the shock, joy, and dancing before the Lord had settled down (you will be reading in the next chapter how this miracle occurred), the Lord reminded me—me of little faith—that I had not trusted Him enough to buy the desires of my heart, what I'd asked Him for.

So, while on the plane home, I repented and asked the Lord to please give me a second chance. I reminded Him that His Father was the God of second chances, that He, too, was gracious, and that if He would again tell me to go ahead—I would do it, and every time in the future. But, I would need to know for certain it was Him, and not me, who was moving ahead. I asked Him for the confirmation when I remembered how the Israelites had been afraid to go into the Promise Land, then they later said they would go, but were destroyed because God did not go with them.

So I waited to know for sure.

Then, on a Sunday afternoon, I could feel the Lord telling me to go to another store. They had the frontload washers and dryers, but with only a six month no-interest. Then He led me to another store where they had twelve months no-interest, and finally, He led me back to the first store where I found that they were running eighteen months no-interest. Though that was good, I just had to know it was God before I purchased them in faith that He was giving me a second chance to act on it.

So, I told the salesman my testimony, and when I told him that it was because I had not asked the Lord, immediately it came to mind to ask the salesman, "Do you think it would be possible to get 24 months no-interest?" to which he replied, "Why not, let me get the store manager and ask him?" When I did ask, he said immediately, "That's no problem at all; be happy to do it!"

Wow, now I had my confirmation, but He was not done. God showed up again in another incredible way. When I got back to that area of the store and told my children who were patiently waiting, my daughter said, "Great, and we *are* getting the black ones, right?" But the black ones were another $300, and even though they did match our other appliances (appliances were in the kitchen, but this was the laundry room!), God was again testing me, so I eagerly said, "Okay" and the salesman wrote up the order.

Now here comes my favorite part...

When I got to the cashier and she looked at the order she said, "Oh, then you are probably going to use your coupon" to which I replied, "What coupon?" and as I looked down, she was sliding a coupon across the counter, and before I could look at it, she rang it up and said, "See! You saved $300!!"

When I looked at the coupon, it said it was for purchasing an appliance on Sunday during a three-hour period. Isn't that amazing?!

It's why He led me around to the other stores, bringing me to purchase them within that small window of time! And yet, why was I so surprised when He is God? And nothing, not one thing, is impossible for Him!

Dear bride, our Father is the God of second chances, and even when we are too afraid to get out of the boat the first time when our Husband calls us, He will give us a second and third opportunity to trust Him and fling ourselves into His loving, giving arms!

Chapter 3

The Power to Make Wealth

"But you shall remember the LORD your God,
for it is He who is giving you power to make wealth,
that He may confirm His covenant which
He swore to your fathers, as it is this day."
—Deuteronomy 8:18

How many of us believe that it is really God who has *given*, yes **given**, us the power to make what we have and have felt we earned?

The message for this chapter: It is God, not our talents nor big breaks nor our education that has given us the power and ability to have everything we own and the money we earn. My goal is to help you, and to reinforce to me, that you and I don't have to do one thing, not one thing, to earn our way in this world. Yes, it goes against all sound thinking, doesn't it? It sounds so spiritually weird that we can't get our minds around it, and even if we could, we are afraid to try for fear of what people would think, and also what really believing this would mean in living our day to day lives.

Does this mean that if today I want to prove God right, I shouldn't show up for work, and that I should write a check for more money than I have in my account? No. I don't think that will prove anything except that we don't have a clue about the difference between stepping out in faith and throwing ourselves off a cliff. It is not the purpose of this chapter to test God—though tithing is the one and only area, the part of our finances (specifically our tithing) when God Himself tells us to test Him, "'Bring the whole tithe into the storehouse, so that there may be food in My house, and **test Me now** in this,' says the LORD of hosts, 'if I will not open for you the windows of heaven and pour out for you a blessing until it overflows'" (Malachi 3:10).

My hope for this chapter, and this book, is for all of us to begin living abundantly, as true daughters of a Heavenly Father who tells us, in Psalm 127:2, that "It is vain for you to rise up early, to retire late, to eat the bread of painful labors; for **He *gives*** to His beloved even in his sleep," when day after day we burn the midnight oil and drag ourselves to work lest we find ourselves in a state of financial lack.

Honestly, I have believed this principle for many years, and yet it wasn't until I was in the place of paying all the bills, facing a mound of debt, without any means of paying for it crumbling below me when I really had a chance to see what I really believed. And to test my faith, as I began sharing in the last chapter, God made sure I had plenty of opportunities, from back taxes I discovered hadn't been paid to me making around the world trips when there was absolutely no money in my bank accounts. Yet God has proved to me time and again that He is more than faithful to be trusted.

It is because our faith is so stunted that it takes many trials, yes, those infamous trials, for our faith to be stretched beyond what we think we can take. I believe I have found what God is looking for, yet even in knowing this, you and I cannot make ourselves come to the place where fear no longer takes hold and grips us—He alone gets us there, gently bringing us to a place of utter and complete trust. And another thing, you and I cannot convince God we have learned what we needed to learn, nor affirm we are free of fear when really we aren't. He can't be fooled; I know because I was the only one fooled when I made this declaration.

What I can tell you is that **it takes a steady dose of crises, mixed with unending trials, with God showing up just in time, then showing up too late, for us to really see and experience the faithfulness of God.**

So why does He bother, or better question, why do you and I bother to continue to strive to experience God's faithfulness, wanting our Husband's intimacy and learning to trust? For me, it's all for one reason—to know Him, to experience Him in every area of my life. Only then will I find true peace and joy, and experience heaven on earth that others will witness and want too. Kind of funny that peace, joy, and heaven on earth have to come through the trials of life, isn't it?

Strange that peace, joy, and heaven on earth are not simply found when we choose the easy road. And no matter how many tests we pass, there, just up ahead, is another narrow gate that the Lord will point out to us and prompt us to take. Why? "For I am confident of this very thing, that He who **began** a **good work** in you [and me] will perfect it until the day of Christ Jesus" (Philippians 1:6).

It has been through these absurd financial trials for me to really experience the utter power and faithfulness of God. Let me define absurd. Ridiculous because it's irrational, incongruous, and illogical. It's illogical because it doesn't follow the rules of logic, does not follow the apparent reasonable, and is not giving us the expected response. To prove this, let's take just one example, like what God says about giving.

God tells us that when we want or need something—this is the time we should give what little we have away. Illogical to be sure, nevertheless, this is the way He created the laws of the universe. And, there is no difference between this principle and the principle of gravity; it is set in place whether we like it or not, or whether we ignore it or not and whether we believe it or not.

Now let me ask again, Who gave us the power to make wealth? Clearly, we have our answer—it's Him.

Financial Testimony #3

"That Building Pledge"

Immediately following my divorce, I had never had more money or more financial blessings! God saw my heart (by my actions and what I said to everyone) when faced with financial ruin, and He began rewarding me according to my faith and trust in Him!

Yet, it was the hidden debt that I was most concerned about when I first took over our family and ministry's finances soon after my husband filed for the divorce. And to help stretch my faith, God chose to use a building pledge that we (my husband and I) had made almost two years earlier to begin increasing my walk of faith. It's funny, but for some odd reason back when we'd made it, I sensed that there was something very significant in our making that particular pledge.

How did I know? Because my husband really balked and resisted "even praying" about making the pledge in the first place; he argued with me about it, even though I never even said a single word. Each time he asked me what I thought, I sought the Lord and immediately was able to respond with a "gentle answer" (that's supposed to turn away wrath, but it didn't). I simply said, "I don't know, why not just pray about it?" and when this wrestling continued, that's when I began to sense that this pledge was significant.

Ladies, any time you see resistance that is out of proportion to what is being discussed, you can be sure that the enemy is lurking close by to try to steal something from you (or your family or your ministry). And this means you can never blame any loss on your husband (or FH), or anyone else since you have the power to keep and gain every blessing through your obedience and trust in the Lord!

After my husband finally threw up his hands, and shouted, "Okay I'll pray!" he returned only minutes later looking entirely different. He had an immediate change of heart and stated he wanted to give a pledge with an amount that was far more than I would have ever dreamed of us giving!! And because I was never included in knowing anything about our finances, two years later, I was totally in the dark as to how much we'd paid towards our pledge. It was only when I was going through the divorce before it was final when they announced one morning in church that the pledges would be due within just a few short weeks.

So, when I saw him, I asked my husband how much we still owed, he said he didn't know, but that I could call the church for the balance. To my surprise, three-fourths (thousands of dollars) were still due! For me to pay this would truly have to come from God—I would need *Him* to make a way.

The significance in this pledge was confirmed over, and over, and over again when time after time after time, my husband kept trying to persuade me *not* to pay it. He told me that **he** had made the pledge, not me, so I didn't need to pay it. He said I should contact the pastor who was over the single moms and widows to ask to be released from it. He told my older sons that if I acted so stupidly I would surely lose everything, including our home, so they too began to reason with me, begging me not to pay it. However, for me, each attempt confirmed that to miss paying this would be a huge loss for me and for our future in regard to our finances.

Let me add something important here: each time my husband spoke to me, we were still married, but since he had moved out and filed for the divorce, each time he told me, I asked him if he was telling me or warning me. Each time he insisted that I needed to make the decision (that he was only concerned and didn't want me to make a mistake that would mean me losing our home—remember, I told you the pledge was a large amount?). And each time I assured him that I would pray about it, which I did. And each time God continued to tell me that He would show me the way.

That is the other point I want to make—there was no way that I could have found a way to pay the pledge, none of it. I was backed up so far to the Red Sea financially already that my heels were getting wet! God had to be the One to do it, which I also kept telling my husband and sons at the end of each of their pleadings with me.

Interestingly, the day that the pledge was due came and went. God still had not shown me the way, but when I prayed, I still sensed God wanted me to seek Him to pay it even if it was late! Then during an evening service, our senior pastor made an announcement that "anyone who had not yet paid the pledge was *released* from what they owed!" Was God telling me that I was released? So I went back into my prayer closet and I asked Him if He was speaking to me through the pastor; yet, once again, He assured me that He would make a way and He wanted me to pay it!

Almost a full month after the pledges were due, God showed me a way!! I honestly was so excited to write the check, and what made it worse, I knew He wanted me to wait another three days for our prayer meeting just so I could put it in the offering! And even then, only two minutes before I was to slip the check into the offering bucket, the enemy had a dear friend lean forward to tell me something to steal the joy I was experiencing as I watched the offering coming down my row!!

Dear reader, it is not until you are pressed in on every side that you truly experience the faithfulness and wonder of God. It was less than three hours later when God blessed me beyond my dreams!! Even now my eyes fill with tears when I think of how awesome God is!!

As I mentioned, just three hours after I put the check in the offering, I received an email from a fellowship member who said that God had laid it on her heart to "sow a substantial seed" into my ministry!! The seed was the EXACT amount of the **entire** pledge!!! Did you see that?? It wasn't only what I had put in the offering just 3 hours earlier, but it was ALL that we gave over the two years—the entire pledge!

But, that is not the end of the blessing. When I called and told my sons, they turned around and called their dad, who then called me (and left me a message on my cell phone) to tell me that I was right and he had been wrong! He told me he was so happy for me. This was huge (as I am sure it would be for you)!!!

As I close this chapter, I hope that what I have shared with you will give you the faith to trust God with everything!! To allow the Lord to so fill you with His love, that it will cast out all fear in trusting your Father to supply all your needs—by stretching your faith in Him through the trials that are meant to show He is faithful.

Remember, too, that you may even see a deadline come and go, but God is not bound by deadlines nor death!! Very often He waits like He did with Lazarus (when he waited for him to be in the tomb and begin to stink) before He shows up! Or like God did with the pledge. His timing is perfect and increases the suspense, gathering more people who are witnessing His faithfulness.

And lastly, if you do have other people who can help you financially, be sure you do **not** go to them for help (and why I kept the financial fate of my situation hidden for so long). Everyone, but God, has a limited supply. Don't sell yourself or your family or your ministry short! Tap into the Father who owns it all and is more generous (and loving) than anyone ever created!! Keep remembering, it was the Father, who sent His Son, who became our Husband and who lavishes us with His love!

"There is no fear in love; but *perfect* **love casts out fear**, because fear involves punishment, and the one who fears is not perfected in love" (1 John 4:18).

Chapter 4

Where Did I Go Wrong?

"'I have done no wrong.'"
—Proverbs 30:20

How many of us think that it had to be something we did *wrong* that caused our current distress? Whether the distress is related to our health, a relationship, or in regard to our finances, we believe that it **had** *to be* our "fault" that this dreadful thing happened.

By blaming ourselves for the mess, however, we have proven a true and humble heart, since the characteristic of the adulteress is that she believes she is *never* at fault. Proverbs 30:20 tell us, "This is the way of an adulterous woman: She eats and **wipes** her **mouth**, and says, 'I have done no wrong.'"

Taking the responsibility for why we are in our present crisis or distress is a great place to start finding our way out—since it leads to us seeking the Lord to search our heart. "Search me [thoroughly], O God, and know my heart! Try me and know my thoughts! And see if there is any wicked or hurtful way in me, and lead me in the way everlasting" (Psalm 139: 23–24 AMP).

However, once you have taken a thorough look at yourself, repented of anything, then it's time to move on to a principle that very few Christians understand. Sadly, even many pastors ignore the principle when preaching. It's understanding that a crisis is often more about God obtaining a greater glory and also for Him to be able to ultimately bless you. Here's the principle in this verse:

"Walking down the street, Jesus saw a man blind from birth. His disciples asked, 'Rabbi, who sinned: this man or his parents, causing him to be born blind?' Jesus said, 'You're asking the wrong question. You're looking for someone to blame. There is no such cause-effect here. **Look instead for what God *can* do**'" (John 9:1–2 MSG).

Our human nature loves to blame someone for the reason when something is wrong. We believe that every problem that plagues us is the result of someone's sin, someone's mistake, someone who is out to get us, when, in fact, it is often God Himself who is behind it. We know this is true because it says so in this verse, "That men may know from the rising to the setting of the sun that there is no one besides Me. I am the LORD, and there is no other, the One forming light and *creating* **darkness,** causing well-being and *creating* **calamity**; I am the LORD who does all these" (Isaiah 45:7).

Yet Christians still refuse to look at this as even a remote possibility; the possibility that it could be God, not just God who is "allowing" this "enemy" attack, but actually God who created the calamity. Yet, if we go beyond the Who and take the next step to "why" then we could fully understand: It is due to God seeking a greater glory, to show the lost (and the believer) what He can do—the impossible.

"Behold, I am the LORD, the God of all flesh; is anything **too difficult** for Me?" "Ah Lord GOD! Behold, You have made the heavens and the earth by Your great power and by Your outstretched arm! **Nothing is too difficult for You**" (Jeremiah 32:27; 32:17)! And finally, "For **nothing** will be **impossible** with God" (Luke 1:37). If you remember, Erin said this verse in Luke is the principle that RMI was founded on, and what keeps it going even now.

So, let me ask you: Why wallow in guilt, or focus on blaming someone else when we are free to move on to the exciting part of each crisis—what also helps to repel fear and shame? Why not look for what God can do and is about to do in our lives when a crisis hits or calamity strikes? Quickly shift the way you think remembering "it was so that the works of God might be displayed"!

Over the past two years, I have felt incredibly blessed because God actually chose *me* to go through some pretty incredible, and often unbelievable trials, in order to allow the works of God to be displayed. So often when trials hit us, we dread, panic, hide, feel guilty, and experience every negative emotion under the sun. Yet, by allowing negative thoughts and feelings to be our focus, which often consumes us, we usually miss the anticipation and excitement of what God is about to do *when* He shows up in our current crisis. And fear can even block what He wants to do, just as Jesus explained in Mark 6:5, "And He [Jesus] could do no miracle there except that He laid His hands upon a few sick people and healed them. And He wondered at their unbelief." The Voice says, "He was amazed by the stubbornness of their unbelief."

Is it stubbornness that causes us to block what He wants to do? Why not just come to a place of utter surrender, no longer wasting time on what we did wrong or blaming others? That's when we will finally understand that God is not interested in *us* fixing our mistakes. So why do we always try to fix something when our Father or our Husband is *about* to show up and do the impossible if we would simply turn everything over to Him?

Therein lies another myth, when Christians tell us "God is never late."

Absolutely, not so.

As I shared in the last chapter, it was after my pledge was due, after the senior pastor said we were released, when God showed me the way to pay it—when a miracle was sent to me from the other side of the earth!

Also, Jesus should be known for being late, and for being late on purpose. "So when He heard that he was sick, He then stayed **two days longer** in the place where He was... So when Jesus came, He found that he had already been in the tomb **four days**... Therefore, when Mary came where Jesus was, she saw Him, and fell at His feet, saying to Him, 'Lord, if You had been here, my brother would not have died.'... Jesus said to her, 'Did I not say to you that if you believe, *you will see the **glory of God**?'"* (John 11:6, 17, 32, 40).

Jesus knew what waiting would do—so He never rushed ahead—He knew it would bring His Father greater glory! Yes, had Jesus gotten there "on time" He would have healed His sick friend and prevented Lazarus' sisters mourning when their brother died. But for Jesus to wait, and be late on purpose, meant that the dead would be raised— proving that God can go beyond what we could ever have believed or comprehended!

The story of Lazarus being raised from the dead, and the fact that Jesus **was late** *on purpose,* is significant to me personally because this is the story the Lord told me to remember when I first sought Him regarding my financial crisis. He spoke this to me the first time when I was in South Africa and just a couple of weeks into a very long and gruelling tour that took me around the world. To my horror, the day before I left for this five-week trip around the world, my bank accounts were totally empty after I withdrew just a very small amount of cash to bring with me! I even hesitated to take the cash out when I saw that by doing so I would have nothing left, but the Lord insisted (as I sought Him).

It is in obeying in the small things (those day-to-day things) that get you to the place of obeying and trusting Him in the big things. If I had not sought Him, and also obeyed what I heard even though it was terrifying to do so financially, I would never have made it to South Africa. When I was ready to leave this country, I found out that I needed that *cash* to get an unexpected visitor's visa to get into Brazil. And to get me ready to believe and increase my faith, even more, I was told at the airport that it would take a full 6 months to get a visitor's visa. Yet only 25 hours after I applied I got mine and got the last seat on that plane! Therein was the first proof that God was in control and would actually begin to use more crises in my life to prove that He was setting me up to eventually bless me. Yes, financially, but the principle stretches into every area of our lives. An incredible principle so few understand, and even fewer are able to make it through because they fail to know or believe what He says. They fail to trust Him in the little things, therefore, when the bigger crises hit, their spiritual muscles are unable to lift or carry the weight of it.

Many of us snicker at the foolish and faithless Israelites, wandering in the desert, people who began to fear at every turn even though they had witnessed first-hand the miracles surrounding the plagues that resulted in their escape from Egypt. And then if that were not enough to build their faith (as we laughingly shake our heads), they even watched the Red Sea become a freeway to the other side. But how can we scoff when so many of us act the same way when we are experiencing far fewer difficulties than they faced? So often we have seen God work miraculously and precisely in so many ways in our lives and in the lives of others. We make reading testimonies a daily habit and yet when He sets us up for the next crisis in our own lives, we immediately suffer from amnesia and entirely forget about His faithfulness—and His timing!

That's why when we begin to stress about His timing (when time is running out) that's when we need to remember that Jesus is often late on purpose—so that God will gain greater glory. Instead of simply healing a sick man, which is commendable, He's late a full four days—four days with a man beginning to stink in a tomb. Each hour more crowds are gathering—when Jesus shows up and shouts, "Lazarus, come forth!" Dear friend, that's the sort of miracle that will rock the world.

By the time I got to South Africa, I could sense that there *had to be* financial trouble back in the States, but each time I tried to get online to take a look at my accounts (that I do regularly when I travel), no matter how hard I tried to get in, God stopped me. It wasn't the internet connection either because I could easily speak with my children, and see them clearly throughout our video chat. But I could **not** get into my bank to see how bad things had become in my bank accounts. Why?

Did you know that God's miracles are usually formed in secret? "My frame was not hidden from You, when I was *made in secret*" (Psalm 139:15). Not only does He want to keep us from concern and many fears that we would experience if we were watching His every move, He also likes to build us up for the big surprise when our miracle appears.

Let me stop here to say that I do know that most expectant mothers have ultrasounds that tell not only the gender of their unborn baby but often detect (possible) abnormalities. Though many of these tests were available even when I was pregnant, I refused to have them, often having to sign a waiver releasing the doctors from any future responsibility or potential lawsuit. After I turned forty, during a pregnancy, I had a Christian doctor who couldn't understand why I refused. She said even if I wouldn't choose abortion, I should want to at least know if my baby would be born with an abnormality in order that I was "prepared." As I was signing the release I simply said, "If something is wrong, He will either fix it, or He'll prepare me." One I didn't take into consideration was Him taking children to be with Him before they could be born with something abnormal, that particular baby girl I lost. Why He wanted her is nothing I need to concern myself with, just knowing He's watching what God determined should be "hidden" is enough for me to trust Him. Over the years I've watched so many mothers who suffered needlessly when they were told anything from being unable to conceive to obvious errors in diagnosis that were *not* present when their babies were born or abnormalities they grew out of (in other words, were healed from).

Please understand I am not saying, nor do I tell anyone to live at this level of faith. You need to crawl before you walk, walk before you run, and practice your faith daily before entering or winning the Olympics. Simple live happily at whatever level of faith you have and trust God to create a variety of calamities to help it increase.

What kept me going then, and what keeps me going now, is to stop looking at how bad things are. Thankfully, most of my bills are done by auto-payments; therefore, I don't have to keep staring at what is happening with my finances. Yes, I could, but I don't. Instead, I look up, into His face, focusing on His goodness and faithfulness—remembering all that He has done for me in the past to keep my faith built up.

The truth is, God did not simply thrust me into this wilderness without first showing me His awesomeness and His faithfulness for many, many years. On two occasions, just recently, God showed me an incredible financial miracle right before my very eyes. The first happened when I had agreed to take on all the family and ministry debt when my husband filed for divorce. It was more than overwhelming since my husband told me honestly that I would not be able to pay all the bills, and due to my giving and stupidity, I would lose our home too.

Since God had taken the time to make me look foolish, to me it was evidence that He was going to do something a bit radical, which meant He'd called me to some sort of radical obedience.

The Lord prompted me to pay thousands of dollars that I told you about in Chapter 1. And as a result, as you also read, a miracle happened. Then, so that I would have *two* financial miracles to remember when things got to the huge crisis I am living now, God allowed me to wake up one morning only to find that I had no money in either of my accounts. It was just after Christmas—how's that for starting the New Year right?

So, let me share this testimony with you; because, guess what? Sharing what God has already done not only can encourage you, but it also keeps me going forward knowing what He is about to do now when I need Him even more! Though I don't know the details of how He'll do it (because if I did, I might become fearful), I do, however, know how it ends!

What He's done, the testimonies I share with you throughout this book were never meant just for me. God set me up, allowing me to live through these trials *for you*—so that you can believe Him for each of your financial crises. And please don't just think of them within the constraints of your finances—each of His principles is good for everything that ails you! Everything that causes you to fear and pull back from moving forward in faith with Him right at your side.

For this crisis, the Lord told me it wouldn't happen immediately and told me to "remember Lazarus." I must be honest, just the thought of me being in a financial tomb and beginning to smell foul (financially) oftentimes makes me feel a bit uneasy or queasy. Yet, each day I wake up and choose to turn those troubled feelings into thoughts of excitement, of a resurrection, rather than a mere healing, which is why He has chosen to make me wait until I am buried.

To be sure, my finances are beginning to smell—oh, but the aroma of an impending miracle! And even though I've done my best to do this quietly, the more people who end up knowing what is happening in my life right now, the more ridiculous, odd or irresponsible I am being accused of. However, this place of being **hopelessly in need of HIM** is the only place I want to be.

Financial Testimony #4

"She Gave Out of her Poverty"

Before I begin, let me lay a foundation. Remember with me the story of the "Widow's Mite" from the Bible, which I shared in an earlier chapter. And just to refresh both our memories, let's read it again, "And He [Jesus] sat down opposite the treasury, and began observing how the people were putting money into the treasury; and many rich people were putting in large sums. A poor widow came and put in two small copper coins, which amount to a cent. Calling His disciples to Him, He said to them, 'Truly I say to you, this poor widow put in *more* than all the contributors to the treasury; for they all put in out of their surplus, but *she,* **out of her** *poverty,* put in all she owned, all she had to live on'" (Mark 12:41-45).

Though I had heard the story many times, it wasn't until I was asked to give when I was in total ruin that I finally understood what it meant to give out of a lack, rather than from an abundance or at least having enough.

It was December, just five months after my divorce was final. God had been incredibly faithful, and I had done my best to be obedient in everything He told me or showed me to do since taking over the family and ministry's finances about eight months earlier.

As I mentioned in my testimony in Chapter One, not only did I take on all that debt, agreeing to no child support, but my ministry was also slowly but surely crumbling. In March of the same year, Erin decided we no longer should minister to men, which accounted for more than 50% of my ministry's income through the book sales; men tended to buy more than women.

The decision to make RMI for women only was posted on Erin's sites and mine the day before my 50th birthday, in March of that same year (my birthday and Erin's are less than a week apart). Once my husband told me about filing for divorce, he suggested that I reconsider not selling our men's resources. Just because of Erin's decision, there was no good reason I should make the same mistake she was making, he said. Yet I knew it had been God who set it up in that order and that He was using Erin, yet again in my life. God knew that my being a newly divorced woman might put me in a vulnerable position if I had anything to do with interacting with helping men who had also lost their wives.

Besides this, using money to make my decisions is a trap. "Do not weary yourself to gain wealth, cease from your consideration of it. When you set your eyes on it, it is gone. For wealth certainly makes itself wings like an eagle that flies toward the heavens" (Proverbs 23:4–5).

So, even before my divorce was final, the men's resources were off my site and my income was immediately cut in half just as RMI's was.

Enter, the next phase of crises.

Even before the divorce was final, the first of several attacks came. But before I go on, please keep in mind that though these attacks came through my ex-husband, there is no point in looking at "who" *your* "enemy" might be. God should be well-known for getting His people into situations where the odds are not in our favor—and He does this purposely! It doesn't matter *who* He chooses to use—please never lose sight of Who creates calamity and for what purpose. He does so to prosper us, stretching us, by allowing us to be put in precarious situations in order for Him to rescue us at the right time, even when that may be late (on purpose).

Though some may debate this fact, there is one place in particular that there is real proof of this principle when Gideon is told to get rid of more and more of his army—cutting his army of 22,000 down to a mere 300. God *purposely* stacked the odds against him knowing that it would be the blasts of the trumpets, not the army fighting, that would win the war. It's the very same with our lives. It's not what we have left, but simply our shouts of praise that will win any battle raging in our life.

So how could I possibly make it when half of my income was gone? Before I had a chance to think about it, God chose to cut my income even further when my husband made more demands. But as I said earlier, it doesn't matter whom the Lord chooses to use. My only reason for mentioning this to you is so you can relate to my story, and let go of all the "details" of your current or future crises. My hope is that you will remember to always keep your eyes on where God is headed and Who is holding your hand. Your Husband.

However catastrophic it became, I was able to see almost immediately that this was the *opportunity* I had been waiting for. For years, I wanted just to GIVE, but I was never in the position of authority to do so. So, now, without needing a husband's permission, I was able to distribute the rest the contents of my bookstore—giving most of it away for free—and the first box I taped shut was sent to Africa! Awesome, right?

However, once the excitement was over, I was left with less and less of an income. Thankfully, I am not the best at handling finances, so I was not aware of how horrific things were becoming. Not until one morning in December. Here, then, is my testimony.

When I woke early that December morning, I was up extra early since I had a lot to keep me busy. It wasn't quite dawn when I went into my online banking and found that both our family and ministry accounts, again, were totally empty. I was online to pay bills, but with no money—that was not going to happen! That's when the Lord spoke to me about cutting the price of the rest of prices in my online bookstore, and then giving a 50% discount to the RMI fellowship members (basically, it meant that it would simply be covering the cost of what I'd paid for them—which meant, I would be getting no profit at all).

No matter how crazy it seemed, I simply thought, "What does it matter anyway since I am basically washed up, ruined?" So, I went ahead, following what the Lord said I needed to do. That same evening, I did another strange thing by answering emails. I never did that (and still don't) since it makes me think too much at night and I can't fall asleep. But that night I did, and that's when I received an email that totally blew me away! Another dear, precious fellowship member of mine, who lives in Asia, wrote to tell me that she was sending a donation of more than fifteen thousand dollars! Read it again. In an instant, God was faithful all because He purposely stacked the odds against me and prompted me to do something ridiculous—give when I really had nothing at all to give. And when I simply obeyed, withholding nothing, He gave abundantly!!

Dear bride, though you may be falling deeper and deeper into debt, God does have a plan and your Husband isn't concerned one bit. Though whatever's happening is nothing that you or I could figure out, we shouldn't even try—not if we want His plan! Just be sure to never, *ever* seek anyone else's help, not ever. Instead, simply wait on God, and be sure to wait even if He's late. Then don't be surprised when things really heat up and you're asked to do something ridiculous.

"Beloved, do not be surprised at the *fiery* ordeal among you, which comes upon you for your testing, as though some strange thing were happening to you; but to the degree that you share the sufferings of Christ, **keep on rejoicing;** so that also at the revelation of His glory [when He comes through for you], you may rejoice with exultation" (1 Peter 4:12).

Though I am in a far more serious situation today than I was even on that day, God has given me (and you) an amazing testimony of what He did not once, but twice. He gave this testimony to us in order for each of us to be ready to be set up for even greater things He wants to do in our lives.

He is our heavenly Husband, after all, the Man who overcame death, and debt, and every other evil of this world. Never forget His promise to us in John 16:33, "These things I have spoken to you, so that in Me you may have peace. In the world you will have tribulation, but take courage; I have overcome the world."

Chapter 5

Hopelessly in Need of Him

"One thing I have asked—
To behold the beauty of the LORD"
—Psalm 27:4

How many of us cringe because of our current financial situation (or any one of our many difficult situations) that are at the level of being considered a crisis in our lives?

Though we cringe at first, it is only when we are in this place of being hopelessly in need of Him when we will really see Him face-to-face! It is when we are backed to the Red Sea, or in the grave for four days and beginning to stink when we truly see the glory of God, right? Then why do we try everything we can to not get ourselves into situations like this and try, in vain, to get ourselves out of these predicaments?

Please don't get me wrong, I am not saying that we should purposely *try* to ruin our finances, or our relationships or our health just so we can see God perform a miracle and witness our Husband face-to-face. What I am wondering is why we "wait until the last moment" before we honestly and fully turn everything over to Him and stop trying to stop the inevitable?

Before any of us are willing to give whatever it is—totally and completely to our Savior, our Husband—we make absolutely sure that we perform at least one or more "last ditch efforts" to save or rescue ourselves. How stubborn we are. "Know, then, it is not because of your righteousness that the LORD your God is giving you this good land to possess, for you are a **stubborn** people" (Deuteronomy 9:6). I don't believe that you and I try to appear stubborn; I believe that we wrongly believe that God will think us foolish or maybe it's that we fear other people (if they knew) would think us irresponsible?

For me, I believe I fall into the last category. No matter how much I try to shake it, what other people think tries to invade my faith. So far I have made it to the point that I am down to just one group of people who concern me, and that group is my children, primarily my older children. However, I'm thankful that I see this concern has diminished or lessening slowly day-by-day as things grow to absurdity in every area of my life, especially financially.

Though I do my best to keep everything to myself (which is a huge change in me since I used to be the one who has always been willing to foolishly "tell all" so that I had everyone else's opinion to help confuse me), I have noticed that when we do our best to be discrete, then the Lord will begin revealing things to others—in order that we are forced to share our faith with them. Have you noticed that too?

Over the course of this year, the Lord continues to put me (and our finances) in very precarious perils, so much so, that invariably I was recently *forced* to reveal what happened to get us to this place and what I plan to do about it. The truth is, there is nothing, really, that I **can** do about my situation. God's plan, in order for Him to receive glory and finish whatever it is He has planned, has put me, us, our family, in an impossible situation on purpose.

"'For I know the plans that I have for you,' declares the LORD, 'plans for welfare and not for calamity to give you a future and a hope'" (Jeremiah 29:11).

When we have an illness, we instinctively do all we can to get healthy, and when we have exhausted our ability to get well, we usually turn to our doctor. If the illness gets worse, we demand more tests, and if unsatisfied, we seek another opinion. It isn't until the doctor finds the "incurable"—the cancer or the inoperable tumor or terminal illness—that we finally fall on our faces before God and surrender it all to Him, putting our entire trust in Him.

Why do we wait until we have exhausted all of our resources, and everyone who we think can help us? Pleading with everyone we know BEFORE we simply put all of our trust in the Lord for what **He** can do?

Is it pride, arrogance, or ignorance? Do we really believe the old saying that, "God helps those who help themselves"? Just for your information, that may be one of the biggest lies that many Christians believe and quote often, but it is **not** in the Bible, nor is there a single principle even close to it. Instead, the contrary is true. Over and over again, God tells us to trust Him and no one else, surely not our flesh or even "leaning" to anything we understand. So, I have begun to choose to trust Him from the onset and fight the feeling that I must have missed Him or grieved Him or should do more to help Him when things continue to get **worse** instead of better.

This is just the point—things have to get worse if we want to draw a Lazarus crowd or see a walkway built through the middle of a sea. These miracles didn't just happen back during biblical times but are happening right now, in all of our lives if we are willing to follow Him.

For me, I love seeing Him face-to-face and watch His glory pass by. I love to need Him to the point that I am desperate for His love. Yes, for me, being hopelessly in need of Him is the recommendation of this writer and for all those who want to be a part of what He is doing in these last days.

Is it scary? Yes! Oftentimes it's very scary. But for each fear, there is a counterbalance of His love that casts out all fear. "There is no fear in love; but perfect love casts out fear, because fear involves punishment, and the one who fears is not perfected in love" (1 John 4:18). He's not punishing you for making a mistake, and certainly not refusing to help you for trusting Him alone.

And just as we have learned in the previous chapters, it's our testimonies that help make us overcomers. "And they overcame him because of the blood of the Lamb and because of the **word of their testimony**, and they did not love their life even to death" (Revelation 12:11).

So, dear Overcomer, here is this chapter's testimony. Forgive me for not sharing them in chrono**logical** order, but I have never been *logical*—I simply am crazy for Him!

Financial Testimony #5

"Honeymoon Bliss"

Can I tell you that I think that God just ROCKS? Yes, it is so true. If you don't feel like dancing most of the time, then you are not thinking about how totally awesome God really is!! "Truly He is my **Rock** and my salvation; He is my fortress, I will never be shaken" (Psalm 62:2 NIV).

I cannot wait to tell you this precious testimony so that you can see that your blessed Savior, your Jesus, your beloved Bridegroom is way ahead of you with blessings that will blow you and everyone else away!!

It was less than two weeks ago when I got a precious phone call from my son who said, "Mom, I have some exciting news, I am getting married!" I was thrilled to hear what I already thought the Lord kept telling me—I was so excited I screamed! Don't you feel like that when the Lord tells you something and then you hear it really happened? Yet when you've got joy, the enemy is just waiting to steal it from you—so be ready.

God has graciously refined me and has seen fit to call me to some really huge feats. Nevertheless, the enemy still tries to tempt us by attacking our feelings, which try to come in and take over. Though thrilled, excited, and in total euphoria, within the hour jealousy tried to make me focus on the fact that my son and his fiancé were visiting with his dad and his new wife. Though this kept knocking at the door of my heart and mind, I chose to go and bolt that door! Making my way into my bedroom to be alone with my Husband, I told Him how I was feeling to which He blew me away!

That's when He reminded me of the plan that we always had regarding our children when they married. My ex-husband and I had purchased a timeshare in order to give our children a honeymoon to reward them for their moral purity. And due to the divorce, and my taking on all the debt, I now had the timeshare (part of the debt I took on), and the credit card, which included all the flying miles that went with it!! Soon after taking on the debt, the Lord made a way for the timeshare to be paid off, and also the credit card too! Isn't it amazing being the bride of such a rich Man?!

Since the beginning of this book I have shared four testimonies with you (this being the fifth), but within each testimony are testimonies. When I took all the debt, the question was why? I am sure there are so many reasons that will appear over the course of my lifetime, but here is just one. Because of my willingness to take the debt, it led to the place of my being able to give something outstanding to my son and my soon-to-be new daughter. This may not mean a lot to you, but I have never been in the position of giving to my children, and now I am thrilled beyond words!

Ladies, when I realized what I had to give, I wanted to pick up the phone right then and call them back to tell them the awesome news!!

Yet, I knew that to call would mean butting into what was going on up there, so thankfully the Lord has taught me the blessings of waiting. I told the Lord to orchestrate *when* I was to tell them.

The opportunity came the next day when my soon-to-be daughter called. I began by asking her if they had made any plans for their honeymoon, and she responded by telling me that they agreed that they could only afford to go to a local vacation village about twenty minutes south of where they lived. And certainly not the honeymoon capital of the world! That's when He led me to share my excitement—I wanted to send them on a week *anywhere* they would like to go! I had the flying miles to just about anywhere, and at a crown level resort for an entire week!

Even now I just have to cry. Here I am in total financial ruin and without my even realizing it, the Lord had graciously run ahead of me and set this whole thing up!!

In total disbelief, she asked *where* they could go, to which I replied, "Wherever! Hawaii, the Caribbean, wherever you two want to go!" Right away she said Hawaii and my son agreed (oh, bless his heart, he has been listening).

Yet, ladies, you know that the enemy is going to try to steal that joy, don't you? Here is how he tried with me.

The next morning he put a terrifying thought in my mind, and then showed it to me—I was short flying miles. Immediately I remembered that I had "turned the other cheek, walked the second mile, giving my coat" with a previous honeymoon I'd given to my ex for him to go to Hawaii and the enemy said, "You fool, now you can't bless your own son!!! You went ahead and gave it away to your unfaithful husband. What a fool!" With this, I ran to the Lord (in my heart and mind), to which He calmed the seas, and said, "Darling, you have the flying miles. Do you think for one minute that I would let you down? Go to your office and look, it's not on this card, it's on the other."

Sure enough, when I went into the files there it was—enough flying miles to get them both to Hawaii and back! That's when the fun began!! With my generous gift offered, soon the talk turned from their honeymoon that I was going to bless them with and them also wanting to get my opinion about everything having to do with their wedding!! The feelings of jealousy for them being with his dad and new wife—turned to joy unspeakable and full, I mean, full of His glory!!

There's more, the news resulted in a very generous counter financial gift from his dad, which proves even more what I have been telling my children over and over again. Not only will my children "not" be destroyed by the divorce, but—God has promised them *double* for this injustice!! How wonderful, how marvellous is my Savior!

"Instead of your *shame* you will have a **double portion**, and instead of humiliation they will *shout for joy* over their **portion.** Therefore they will possess a **double portion** in their land, everlasting joy will be theirs" (Isaiah 61:7). I heard later that my ex-husband's new wife would not be "outdone" so it was she who offered the sizable financial gift from her account. Isn't that just too wonderful for words?!?!

Back to the honeymoon: I know this is getting long, but each detail is a testimony in itself, and if you are like me, you love to hear it all—"Don't sum it up—tell me everything!!"

The moment they got home, the first thing they did was to sit down with me while I called to make the arrangements for the resort. Oh, I wish I had more time, but here is the best part of it. When I called, they said that to ask for a resort in Hawaii during a red week, and because it was just three months away, was "**ridiculous.**" To which I kept replying "I don't understand."

At first, I really didn't understand the way she was explaining it, but then I did understand what she was saying. She was saying "You're foolish to even ask; it's impossible." Yet when I sought the Lord as she was telling me the same thing over and over, He just kept telling me to hang in there, don't give up, just keep asking. So I did.

Finally, exasperated with me, she asked me to hold on. There was no music so I figured that she had hung up on me; it's happened before, lots of times, so I thought I should hang up and try again, but the Lord said, "Just wait." Finally, she got back on and said that she found something that I could exchange—the first miracle.

Next, I had to contact another company to find an exchange. Once again, the man kept telling me of the impossibility, but I am a personal friend with the One who does the impossible. In fact, I became His bride on July 1, 2005!

In total shock the man said, "Hey, wait a minute. Here is something." On the exact island where they wanted to spend their honeymoon, AND in a one-bedroom unit (not a studio) that I had asked for, there was one that was available on the exact day I asked!!

Though we knew it was a miracle, God even used this man who was in Mexico City to tell us that it just "doesn't happen—this kind of thing just doesn't happen" to which I was able to happily reply "It does when you trust God, as a matter of fact, it happens all the time!" Though you and I know and experience this kind of thing happening all the time, I just never want to get used to it! I want it to keep me in total awe and completely in love with the One whom I owe everything!

Though we are right in the midst of this entire testimony (for there is still more to come), let me end with this that just thrills me!!

The cost of this incredible miracle is *more,* yes more than the entire wedding is going to cost!! Is that God or what?? Here I am, in "apparent" and utter ruin, and yet (because of my Husband going before me) I am able to bless this young couple with the honeymoon of their dreams!

And as I said earlier, the enemy keeps trying to steal my joy. Just a day later my oldest son casually mentioned that he was going to marry this year, to which the enemy bombarded my mind with, "See, you fool, now you don't have enough flying miles for your oldest son; the son that helped you the most" and on and on the enemy goes.

But you know what? I know that God has that all worked out too. The only thing I need to do is resist falling into the Poverty Mentality that says "I won't or don't have enough" when God has promised to provide **all** of our needs, that He longs to be gracious to us, and that He will give us the desires of our hearts when we delight ourselves in HIM.

If you're in the midst of being hopelessly in need of Him—you're in a perfect place for a miracle. Don't waste your time trying to figure out how, or miss one second of the joy that God has waiting just for you when you trust Him with your finances. Believe that you are rich even when your bank accounts say otherwise—this is that faith that is hoped for but is presently unseen.

———— Chapter 6 ————

Obedience Rather Than Sacrifice

"Behold, to **obey** is better than **sacrifice**"
—1 Samuel 15:22

"Samuel said, 'Has the LORD as much delight in burnt offerings and **sacrifices** as in **obey**ing the voice of the LORD? Behold, to **obey** is better than **sacrifice**, and to heed than the fat of rams'" (1 Samuel 15:22).

"Because you have burned **sacrifices** and have sinned against the LORD and not **obey**ed the voice of the LORD or walked in His law, His statutes or His testimonies, therefore this calamity has befallen you, as it has this day" (Jeremiah 44:23).

There is a lot to learn from the mistakes of others; especially beneficial is learning from the mistakes we make ourselves.

Just recently I was blessed when I got an email from my oldest son about a financial crisis that had happened to him. He emailed me because he wanted some wisdom about what to do. Yes, I was honored, but before getting puffed up I had to first laugh because what a joke it is that he had asked **me**—due to my present situation. Nevertheless, I was honored and sought the Lord for what wisdom He wanted me to share with my son.

One of the first things my son thought he should do (and told me, so I wouldn't be surprised) was to sell his very beautiful car. If you are one of RMI's fellowship members, then you may remember I shared in a praise report about the car that the Lord blessed him with just a little over a year ago. Both of my sons were blessed with new cars (that they had each been praying for) that came in the Lord's normal fashion, a crisis, when for three months in a row (mine was the third) there was a car accident (none were our fault) that resulted in my sons' cars being "totalled," which led to new cars for each of them (mine resulted in damage to me only, leading me to minister to a recent widow and her son). By far the most severe accident was my oldest son's, which everyone said looked *worse* than most *fatal* car wrecks!

Due to these accidents, we all witnessed God's mercy, His love, and His way of doing things in a new and amazing way: the cars that each of my sons got were proportionate to the accident that happened. My oldest son was blessed with a car of his dreams that cost him half of what it was worth. This was due to an "error" at the car dealership that they said was "too late" to change and so they said he was extremely "lucky"—he's blessed.

When my son told me that selling his car was what he planned to do to help with his financial crisis, I told him that I doubted that this is what God was telling him to do. Instead, we discussed some of God's principles—one of the most important being that God wants our *obedience* rather *than our sacrifice.*

There's no doubt it would be a sacrifice to sell his car, and that his sacrifice would not impress God. How often have we tried to do something to make things right, only to find that we are in the same or a worse situation?

What kind of obedience was I talking about? Instead of sacrificing, learning to obey God's principles in regard to his dilemma, in other words, what does God say in His Word regarding our money? Here are just a few principles I shared with my son:

Tithing: never steal from God. God asks us to give Him back 10% of what He gives us, and depending if you want to be blessed on your gross or net, tithe on that. Make sure, too, that you tithe to your storehouse, where you're spiritually fed.

I confessed to my son that the moment I took over the finances in our family and ministry, I realized that I gave a larger tip of 20% when I went out to eat than I gave to Him! I told him from that moment on, I began giving that much to God because I wanted God to know that He means more to me that a server at a restaurant or the lady who does my nails. That is not sacrifice to do so; this is actually when we are mature enough to begin to give Him offerings.

"Will a man rob God? Yet you are robbing Me! But you say, 'How have we robbed Thee?' In **tithes *AND* offerings.** You are cursed with a curse, for you are robbing Me, the whole nation of you!" (Malachi 3:8–9). So, I encouraged my son to ask God where to give a 10% offering just as He'd been faithful to show me.

Now let me quote from one of Erin's books, in it, she says:

Laws of Creation: you must understand and obey the Laws of Creation. God set the entire universe into motion with physical laws like gravity, and spiritual laws like tithing. When you find that you have a lack of funds, that's when you need to look at your life to see if you have violated any of those laws. If you fail to give to the *storehouse,* where you are spiritually fed, then God can't rebuke the devourer because we failed to obey His laws.

"'Bring the whole tithe into the storehouse, so that there may be food in My house, and test Me now in this,' says the Lord of hosts, 'if I will not open for you the windows of heaven, and pour out for you a blessing until it overflows. ***Then* I** will **rebuke** the **devourer** for you, so that it may **not destroy** the fruits of the ground; nor will your vine in the field cast its grapes,' says the Lord of hosts" (Malachi 3:10–11).

The devourer is running havoc in many Christians' lives as they watch their homes and lives fall apart. Their car or appliances are breaking and so are their relationships. If you try to keep fixing things in your life, without realizing where the root of the problems lay, the problems will continue. By simply following this basic rule of tithing to your storehouse and then growing spiritually so you then can begin giving above your tithe of 10% (giving at least as much as we tip those who serve us), you will save yourself hours of worry and you will have turned your life from a life of trials to a life of blessings—until your blessings overflow!

Give and it shall be given. This is by far, especially lately, one of my most favorite principles. Wow, get a hold of this one and your life will immediately be one of abundance! "Give, and it will be given to you. They will pour into your lap a good measure—pressed down, shaken together, and running over. For by your standard of measure it will be measured to you in return" (Luke 6:38). Rather than give, especially when we are in need, we withhold and come to more lack in our lives. It doesn't just mean giving financially, but in every area of our lives: relationships, friendships, patience, and love. Most women care more about these emotionally based needs, except, that is when we find ourselves in need of money—then our lack of money begins to take center stage.

"There is one who scatters, and yet increases all the more, and there is one who withholds what is justly due, and yet it results only in want. The generous man will be prosperous, and he who waters will himself be watered" (Proverbs 11:24–25).

Storehouse sits empty. Because most Christians are ignorant of God's principles they unknowingly violate the laws of God to their own destruction. In Hosea 4:6 it says, "My people are destroyed for lack of knowledge. Because you have rejected knowledge..." One of the main focuses of many churches and many Christians, when they speak, is that of fighting with the devil, when in fact, the One whom they are fighting is actually the Lord of hosts.

"'You look for much, but behold, it comes to little; when you bring it home, **I blow it away.** Why?' declares the Lord of hosts, 'Because of My house which lies desolate, while each of you runs to his own house'" (Haggai 1:9).

Let me share something a bit sad. There are only a handful of women who keep RMI going, I know because I've helped with the bookkeeping. Only a very few women tithe so that everyone else can have spiritual food, and just about none of the men. In addition, only a handful of ladies, who, by the way, are the same ones who sow their tithe, also give their time and energy as volunteers. AND these are the very same women are who also the same who submit the most praise reports. Any correlation?

Of course! These women are the ones whom the Lord blesses the most because each and every one of His principles works! The men have just about no restored marriages, very little praise, and it's simply because our society of women has become the only partner in the relationship who give to it!

Also, what's extremely important is that if you are not giving to your storehouse, which most often is RMI, then you are not battling with the enemy, but with the Lord of hosts. We do hear often that our men tithe to their church, even though RMI is feeding them, and this is another confirmation that God does care where you tithe. The offering is where you can give somewhere else, like giving an offering to your church if that's where He leads you. Just make no mistake, God does care about the details and the only person you're fooling is yourself and deceiving those who are watching your life.

Second Corinthians 3:2 NASB, "You are our letter, written in our hearts, known and read by all men." If you profess to be a Christian, His follower, but your life is riddled with lack and loss, then what everyone is learning about God and being a believer, is that it's better not to be.

Yet, when you learn that to give is more blessed, and you begin to practice this principle in every area of your life, then your life becomes abundant! That's the way the entire universe was set up. And this is what everyone will also be a witness to. If, however, you continue to take or withhold, and that is your focus, then I can say without even knowing you that you are miserable and in constant need—in all areas of your life. And that may explain why none of your loved ones want to know more about the One who you want them to know.

Power to make wealth. When we are lacking funds, rather than checking to see if we have violated a spiritual law, we instead do as the non-believer does, we try to think of ways we can "earn" more. This is also due to ignorance because God says, "It is vain for you to rise up early, to retire late, **to eat the bread of painful labors;** for He *gives* to His beloved even in his sleep" (Psalm 127:2).

Why? "Otherwise, you may say in your heart, 'My power and the strength of **my hand made me this wealth.'** But you shall remember the Lord your God, for it is **He** who is *giving you* power to make wealth . . ." (Deuteronomy 8:17–18). Working hard only makes you tired, but it rarely helps you to get ahead of your debt. It is *only* when we look to the Lord, in all areas of our lives, that we find a "yoke that is easy and that burden that is pleasantly light"! (Matthew 11:29).

Stop worrying. "And which of you *by worrying* can add a single hour to his life's span? If then you cannot do even a very little thing, why do you *worry* about other matters? Consider the lilies, how they grow: they neither toil nor spin; but I tell you, not even Solomon in all his glory clothed himself like one of these. But if God so clothes the grass in the field, which is alive today and tomorrow is thrown into the furnace, how much more will He clothe you? You [wo]men of little faith!" (Luke 12:25-28).

Just recently I have found that I have fallen into a very bad habit of believing that I cannot "afford" something if it isn't priced outrageously cheap. This is due to the fact that God has anointed my spending power when I shop for anything! I am known to get the most unbelievable bargains, and not because I am a bargain shopper (that a young man accused me of). Instead, when I need something the Lord always leads me to a particular store, and once in the store, I ask Him what He wants to show me. Simple enough.

The fact that I continually get something, often for less than it costs the store, caused me to think inaccurately—I began to think "cheap" was all I could "afford." What I came to realize is that God does not want us to believe we can only "afford" something that is greatly discounted, but instead, this is how we can **confirm** what He wants us to purchase. Do you see that it's the heart that's different? Here are a couple of examples of when I got it right.

My daughters were asked to be in the upcoming wedding (that you read about in the last chapter; when my son got engaged). The youngest will be a junior bridesmaid, so the dress that the bride chose for her other bridesmaids would not fit her properly since she is a tween—not enough up top to fill it out. The bride told me she found a similar dress where she ordered her wedding dress, so it was discounted from $99 to $79.

Keep in mind that my finances are beyond crisis, so the enemy wants my emotions to result in panic; however, I know God's principles, His love, and His longings. Therefore, I choose, daily, to keep my emotions in the framework of *expectation* rather than *dread* or *fear*. (Remember, I have daughters who need dresses and I am the mother of the groom!)

So, I told her that I believed that the Lord had something else in mind, not because it wasn't affordable, but because she also added right at the end that it didn't fit "all that well." I assured her that if I hadn't found something in a week's time, I would run in and order the one she had found.

Ladies, because I could sense God wanted to do something, I didn't even have to leave my home for Him to move, which was due to my faith and HIS love. A couple of days later the bride called me with excitement that she had found a better dress for half the price, then her cell phone died. An hour later my son called to tell me that she left there, went to another store and found the most perfect, and adorable dress for just $18. I never wondered if it would fit because I knew that God had gone before us and had that dress there just for my daughter. Sure enough, when she got home it fit beautifully!!

That blessing turned to yet another blessing when I headed to the same two stores at the suggestion of the bride. At the first store, I found nothing but continued to ask the Lord where to go. He led me to the second store and immediately after walking in, I found the exact blouse that I had described to my daughters that I wanted to go with a skirt I had but had never worn. I purchased it for only $13.35, which was originally $190. The same scenario happened with my daughter's shoes!

A week later the Lord laid on my heart to buy my oldest son's "soon to be fiancé" a winter coat. Please keep in mind that anyone looking at my finances would scold me and tell me to not even think about giving anyone a gift when I have no money. Nevertheless, when I walked into the store I spotted a shoe sale and told my daughter that we would find the shoes for the wedding there— after we bought the coat that I also knew was there. Sure enough, she did for just $20! Shoes originally sold for over a hundred dollars!

Once again, this is not because of *how* I shop for bargains, but the heart that I have regarding shopping. I am not afraid to purchase something even in the depths of financial lows, but I don't go out to test God either. I simply have the faith and live the principles that He set in motion. Living these principles creates abundance and overflowing, or violating them results in lack and disappointment.

Begging bread. "I have been young and now I am old, yet I have not seen the righteous forsaken or his descendants **begging bread**" (Psalm 37:25). Honestly, this prophet might witness something else if he were living today. We might not necessarily be begging "bread" but we do beg others to help us financially—I know because I was one of them when I went seeking a loan. (More on this in a later chapter since that testimony is currently being written in my life.)

Conclusion? After I shared these and a few other principles with my son, he shared that he was living most of them, but in regard to trying to earn, rather than simply giving as a source of being blessed, he said was something he always did but couldn't do recently because he was trying to work harder to get some more money (something we all do). So, he said what he was going to do after he hung up was to ask the Lord where he needed to give, no longer focusing on making money and that he'd reconsider selling his car.

Finances have since turned around for my oldest son, and he kept his car for eight more years! I hope that you too will take hold of God's laws and choose to follow them by speaking to your Heavenly Husband and allowing Him to bless you. Do not be frightened about purchasing something, and always focus on giving.

And now, just to give you another testimony to help solidify what God can do when you *obey* His spiritual laws rather than *sacrifice* what He has not asked for, I find it amazing that the testimony that I had planned to share with you is about my oldest son and a blessing that will last a lifetime!

My Sixth of Many Financial Testimonies

"Getting Engaged"

In the last chapter, I was blessed to share about the honeymoon I was able to bless my son with. Well, as I have shared many times in many of my books, God promises us that we will receive double! When my oldest son found out that his younger brother was engaged he had a strange expression on his face. After drawing out the truth, I came to find out that he and his girlfriend had planned to marry the weekend just before, but had not announced anything due to the fact that they didn't have the money to buy her an engagement ring.

The couple then had to discuss (after many tears on her side) that it would be wrong to get married before his brother and take the focus away from them. God saw their hearts and was about to bless them beyond imagination.

While going to order one of the bridesmaid dresses (that I mentioned earlier in this chapter), the lady sent me across the store, when about midway I heard the Lord tell me to turn around. I turned and tried to see what He wanted me to look at when I spotted a jewellery counter that had a blue sign that said: 60% off and a red sign on top of that one that said: "Take an additional 30% off." Yes, I immediately did the math and headed to the counter. I didn't even know *why* I was there or what "I" needed, but then my oldest son came to mind.

My daughters and I found a beautiful ring that was so inexpensive it was ridiculous. So, I excitedly called my son and told him to get down to the store and get it. He told me he "just didn't have the money," so I asked him "what about all the clients you have," but he said that they hadn't paid him yet.

It wasn't until the next morning when a fellow RMI member wrote and blessed me and gave an outrageously generous donation that God convicted her of giving me when I realized that I was one of my son's clients who hadn't paid him!

Soon after my return from my last trip to Africa, I was supposed to pay the second half of an e-commerce site my son had built for me. When I told him I didn't have the money to pay (back then), he did, in fact, tell me not to worry about paying it. He said that I had already blessed him and his company so much to get started by motivating them, that I never had to pay the final half of the bill.

Then, just before the New Year, Erin let me know that he and his company had tithed to RMI, and I saw it was more than what I had owed him. That morning, God, in an instant, had convicted me that I was indebted to him, which turned to utter joy at the thought of blessing him with the ring I saw!

When I called to shout the praises on my cell phone—that he probably would have been able to hear miles away from where he lived because I was so happy, I instead heard myself calmly ask him to meet me at a coffee café just outside the mall.

While there I explained how God had convicted me, and that I was there to buy him an engagement ring, but added that I wasn't sure if it was what his fiancé would like. Then he pointed to the jewellery store where they had picked out the ring she wanted. Can you believe that out of my mouth, on the phone, I asked him to meet me just outside the exact jewellery store where the ring they chose was?!?

So, we went in to look at that ring and then went to the other store to see the ring I had found the night before. We soon realized that the main diamond was not the same cut, but nevertheless, I knew her ring was in that case! (It was my younger teenage daughter who assured me that it had to be the ring when I set off that morning.) After looking at two rings—there it was—it looked just like the one my son had just shown me—only this one had bigger diamonds, and **and** included the wedding band (that also possessed a line of diamonds)!! The only difference was that it cost one-fourth of what he would have paid (had he been able to purchase it). Therein lies another principle: until we learn to follow His leading, we will find that He blocks a purchase because He has something better in mind when we *finally* seek Him for help.

God allowed me to bless my son for the thousand ways that he has blessed me—and my ministry. It was my son who got me up on the Internet, and it was he who convinced me that I'd be able to write books about what God was doing in my life. He is the one who had my books ready to be printed. And as I have said to him, and now want to say to you—if it were not for my son giving me the confidence and lending me his support, I would never have my own ministry. Yes, Erin and RMI are the first whom God used to turn my life around. But if not for my son, I know I would not be able to minister to anyone. I would still be a local speaker at a few women's meetings at our church. Well, maybe not after my husband (his father) left again. Yet, again, it was my son who encouraged me to accept the first speaking engagement outside this country after his dad left us.

It wasn't until my son had the ring in his hand when we turned the corner, that he took hold of my arm and with tears in his eyes thanked me, almost unable to speak. My oldest son is not in the least emotional, so to see him so moved was something I will never ever forget. He told me that after my call the night before, he went to his room and with his face to the ground, he cried out to God to help him get a ring. Yes, like Erin loves to say, "I [too]have **no greater joy** than this, to hear of my children walking in the truth" (3 John 1:4).

Today, this very evening, something special will take place in the Big Apple, New York City. My son will ask a beautiful young woman to be his wife and hold out that very special ring—hoping to make her his bride.

Chapter 7

Cornered

"For Pharaoh will say of the sons of Israel,
'They are wandering aimlessly in the land;
the wilderness has shut them in.'"
—Exodus 14:3

Today while returning home from a dentist's appointment, I had a chance to share some truth with my daughter that I would love to share with you too. It encouraged me while I was encouraging her. Today, if you are feeling a bit *cornered* in your current situation, I believe, you, too, will walk away encouraged. Here is what I said:

Did you know that the sheer absurdity of some of our situations is a clear sign that the Lord is doing something amazing in our lives? Our current crisis, especially the more **il**logical, is happening for one very good reason—it's in order that He can build an awesome testimony. A testimony that He hopes we will share to encourage others, and more importantly, to help them know Him in a deeply personal relationship—a relationship that "begins" with their salvation.

Testimonies are wonderful to have, yet they are never easy to live *through*. The little crises that we get through *easily* are rarely good enough to excite most people into seeking the Lord for themselves. The little testimonies we can easily travel *through* certainly wouldn't mesmerize any group of women I've met in Kenya, or Brazil. So that's why the Lord saw fit to begin building some incredible testimonies for me to share—knowing I would be traveling someday—sooner than I ever expected.

Whether or not I go back around the world again, or whether or not you will soon venture into a new country you never even knew existed, the Lord is all about building almost unbelievable testimonies in the lives of His brides. Also, I can personally attest to the fact that without having a Husband to take my hand, and carry me over the rough spots, most of my trials I'd never have made it *through*—which is always the key focus of my testimony—Him, His love and how He carries us over the thresholds of new things too difficult for us.

Another reason our trials are so difficult is that in today's world we also are competing with television shows and movies, viral posts. Television and YouTube videos claim to be "reality" but are in "reality" situations that are most often setup and staged, fictional, to capture its audience. That's why the Lord is doing even greater feats of amazement in the life of His brides. A bride who is so in love with Him that she is willing to trust Him, allowing Him to foster a desire for other women (and men) to seek to find Him and His love.

So, is this what's going on in your life dear bride? Does your life appear to be so incredibly, and horrendously fictional due to the crazy trials that you are being asked to go through?

That's just what's been going on in my life and in our family since the Lord chose to begin building a new testimony in my life: when my husband walked out on our restored marriage. There are many, many areas of my family's life that we went *through:* tremendous crises, trials, attacks, and betrayals—honestly, the list is endless. It seemed that the "enemy" was coming against me in every area of my life: my relationships, my reputation, my ministry, my finances, and also coming against my children. Nevertheless, while writing this particular book I have tried to stay focused primarily on our financial crises and how He brought me *through* them.

Yet, questions tried to pound in my brain, not just from the enemy but from people who would ask: How could any man do what he did to his family? Stating, that by leaving me and our children he had to have known that it would cause mass destruction—since he'd already done it once before. How could he sleep at night?

So, my question to my Beloved was: Is my ex-husband a man of the worst kind, since the actions of these kinds of men are actually destroying their own children in pursuit of their personal gain? Or are we looking at this entirely wrong?

Didn't the Bible tell us that it was *God* who hardened Pharaoh's heart? And if He hardened Pharaoh's heart, then does it really matter *who* is behind the crisis you and I are currently living through? And if it wasn't God who hardened my ex-husband's heart, or your bosses' heart, or that friend you thought you could count on and trust, but instead it was their *own* selfishness, and self-centeredness, may I ask: Who besides me would have to confess that if it were not for the Lord and His love, now as His bride, you and I would act the very same way?

Now, getting back to the point, if God had not used a Pharaoh and his army to corner the Israelites, then would any of us have witnessed the parting of the Red Sea? And if we didn't have the testimony of the Red Sea, how would we be able to believe God and His promises in our situation?

That's what my daughter and I were just discussing today. It came up because we had just come from a consultation where her dentist told us that once we were through (in the matter of a few weeks), her treatment was going to cost thousands of dollars. And because of the guilt my daughter had, that I (as her mom and only provider) had to pay it, my daughter went to the bank, emptied her savings account, and put a stack of money in my hand to help pay for it.

We are all just like that with God, aren't we? We are so indebted to Him, and feel too guilty to accept His free gift, so we feel that somehow, in some way, we need to do "something" to help. Yet, just like my daughter, our attempts to help are so feeble since our resources and abilities are *limited* while His are **limitless**. It is just so difficult to fathom the goodness of God, of His generosity, because we feel unworthy to accept it; don't we?

At this moment, I am seeking the Lord about accepting her money since I don't want to rob her of a blessing. Yet, even more importantly, I don't want to encourage her to believe that she must help God when He puts her in a position of needing Him, and Him alone.

Currently as I've stated over and over—I am being backed into the Red Sea financially, and the deeper I get, the harder it has become, becoming nearly impossible, to hide it any longer from my children. My children and I have all come to know that basically—there is really no way out. Often, when I really think of how bad things are, or have to look at how horrible things are (when I pay a bill or look at my bank balance), my mind wants to do SOMETHING!! And each time the Lord poses the same question, "Michele, what *can* **you** do?" Truly my situation is so much more than anything I could ever do, so it's simply foolish for me to even try. Therefore, I choose to simply trust Him.

What could the Israelites do when the enemy had them *cornered* next to the Red Sea, shut in on every side?

In the same way, how can my daughter help? What she can do to help is much too little, and much too late. We all must face that our entire family is being buried in insurmountable debt with no way out. Funny thing is, I knew that we would be.

When I first began to watch our finances fading, the Lord told me to remember Lazarus, and immediately I thought: That guy was buried, right? But not before He died. So my question to the Lord then and something I ask often is, "Am I dead, or am I already dead and am I being buried?" I ask because I am looking beyond where I am to when His resurrection power arrives! I am waiting to hear Jesus calling out to me, like He did for Martha and Mary's brother—"Lazarus, come out!" with that loud voice that I listen every day to hear.

The absurdity of my situation—no one would believe it if they knew the details—but it is the truth. That's why I know that it *has* to be God. So when I began to weaken in my faith this past Sunday, He was so faithful to make sure I knew it was Him so I was spiritually solid to face the next day.

When I woke up Monday morning I had to rush my son over to urgent care, and as you might expect, we have no medical insurance. Two hours later I got home, only to run my daughter to the dentist who referred her to an endodontist for a root canal (and we all know how expensive that is). Then when I got home I got a call from our orthodontist to get an x-ray for my son's wisdom teeth to be removed. And, yes, of course they need to come out. Within a matter of ten hours, I was being buried in even more debt than I or anyone could imagine.

That same day I found myself pleading with my daughter to NOT ask her dad to pay for her dental work. Even though she didn't come right out and ask him, she gingerly let her step-mom know about what's going on, and she found out that the news had reached her dad. Though it surprised my daughter that he didn't offer to help, and that instead he indirectly boasted that *he* now had dental insurance and that his new bother-in-law is a dentist—it didn't surprise me he didn't offer to help. That's because all of what's happening is part of His plan, a plan to prosper us! If her dad helped (or if anyone else helped), wouldn't it take away from what He is about to do?

Yet, later, I had to ask myself *why* I hadn't just let her go ahead and plead with her dad to help? Didn't we need the help? Didn't he *owe* it to her—I mean, she's his daughter too. But I know why. It's because either my God *will* supply ALL our needs or He won't. And if He won't, what am I doing trusting Him for my salvation. I mean—that's for eternity!!

Isn't that the point? Either we can trust the Lord in **all** areas of our lives, or it's ludicrous to trust Him for something as permanent as forever, right? We're talking eternity! In addition, let's talk about **us** *helping* God. Doesn't "God help those who help themselves" or did He instead say that it is "not by works of righteousness (since they are filthy rags), but according to His mercy that He saved" and is continually saving us as we cry out to Him?

And if we do have to help Him, isn't that works? Doesn't that mean **we,** then, can boast? And if it is our works that are needed, then what about that sweet Mormon girl that I have been witnessing to—her "religion" is a pretty good one as religions go. Is the Good News message to simply trust the Lord *initially,* but then **work** like crazy to gain a higher place with Him, like keeping the Sabbath, don't drink caffeine, etc, etc.?

How can I honestly tell this Mormon girl that trusting Him alone is enough, if my life proves that He can't be trusted to provide **all** of our needs without a little help (or worrying) from me?

Maybe this all sounds too ludicrous for you, but it is making so much sense to me.

Yes, fear tries to grip me.

Reason tries to confuse me.

Doubt tries to invade that peace that I have grown so accustom to.

So I dig my fingers deeper into that spear-pierced side of His, and grab any part of His garment that I can find. If I don't have Him, truly, who do I have? And when it comes down to it, what do I want or need besides Him anyway? This house, a ministry, my reputation?

Dear bride, whether you are under piles of debt, or shame, or fear, or ridicule, or emotional scars, or physical pain—you, my dear, are being *cornered* on purpose. He wasn't worried when this all began, and He is not concerned now that it has taken a sudden turn for the worse. It is all part of the glorious plan that He foreknew and preplanned long before you were even born. And all of it, my love, is for a purpose. But the greatest purpose is so that you, whom He adores so much, can experience His immeasurable love for you, and unlimited patience, toward you.

Dear friend, if you are facing anything like I am, do what I plan to do—crawl deep into His mercy and His grace, then look up and peer intently into His face of glory that reflects the goodness that is about to happen.

My Seventh of Many Financial Testimonies

"Honeymoon Bliss, Continued"

In chapter 5, I shared with you how the Lord miraculously had gone before me and set up a honeymoon that was a dream for a young couple. And as I mentioned, the enemy is always out to steal our joy if he can't first steal our miracle. He is able to steal it when we panic and agree with him when the blessing looks like it won't happen.

The day I wrote the final paragraph of the honeymoon testimony, I was able to finally get the exact dates of the resort so that I could book the flight. Since I know how *delay* in anything brings in new obstacles, I was somewhat expecting something. Yet, this one crisis helped to stretch my faith and has since given me a new and exciting outlook that I had not been able to grasp had it not been for this test.

While booking the flight online, it finally occurred to me that the dollar amount that was on the screen was **above** and *in addition* to the 80,000 flying miles I had. What threw me off was that the second two options had a higher dollar amount; so I assumed that the amount posted simply meant the "cost of the flights" if a person were paying for them, **not** that it was adding additional money I had to *pay!*

That's the moment the enemy held a party in my honor. The enemy mocked me, reminding me how I had been so excited to tell *everyone* how good God is, and what a joke my testimony was that I had just written. Now, here I was, once again, the biggest of fools. He reminded me over and over again that I was going to have to pay hundreds of dollars that I did **not** have. "Now what are you going to do 'foolish woman of God'"?!?!

What else could I do? All I could do was to tune into the still small voice of the Lord. Except, when fear takes hold, it deafens you to hearing from Him. I wonder if this is how Eve felt? When the enemy lied to her, did her heart sink to the point that she was made deaf to what she already knew about the goodness of God? I think that maybe for the first time I am finding compassion and understanding with the first woman and mother of mankind.

Though it seemed like an eternity, I believe the miracle happened within about 24 hours of trusting Him with this crisis. It took my digging deep into my faith to choose to move ahead. I told myself, "Okay, so what? If I have to pay, I will pay it. Never mind about the testimony that is now not as good as it was. I, at least, got it down on paper, right? If I don't share it again, that's okay. Or if I do, of course I would explain the "little P.S." at the end. P.S. I had to pay several hundred dollars. For a honeymoon in Hawaii it's still a great deal, right?"

Right before I was getting online to book it, I decided I need to build my faith, so I began going over **all** that the Lord had miraculously done in my life. Even the most recent things He's done, when you stop to ponder them, will build your faith in His ability to "work all things out for good" and do the impossible! It was during this period of complete bombardment in my mind that I realized that I needed to be sure to write and post each and *everything* the Lord did for me, then print it off and keep it in a single document so I can search for as much encouragement as I will need the next time I'm going through crisis. Something to hold onto and read during times like these. And along with these testimonies of my own, I also plan to gather ones from our the RMI website of faithful brides, like you, also any I can write down that my friends have shared with me. I must continually build enough faith so that no crisis can ever come against to topple me, not ever! But, first, let me finish my testimony.

Just before I logged onto the site, I found myself asking the Lord to "reduce" the additional cost. The first thought I had was to ask Him to "eliminate" it, but my faith could only truly believe for a "reduction." So that is what I asked Him for.

When I opened the page, instead of three options, there suddenly appeared a fourth that was not there the other four times I had logged on!!! And it was the lowest cost that was listed first! Rather than hundreds of dollars, which I didn't have, suddenly the additional cost was just $61.00. Remember, I asked for a "reduction" —so the Lord gave me just what I had asked for!!

Elated, I shared it with all my children who were just in the next room. However, booking it was still proving to be a brick wall, which leads me to another principle: To gain your blessing it often takes *pressing through*. No matter how often I tried, the site wouldn't take my information and ultimately I had to seek God for wisdom. He told me to call, which did mean I was starting all over. Which leads to another principle:

The enemy not only loves to *steal* our promise, and our joy, but when that won't work, he loves to **wear** us out. "He will speak out against the Most High and **wear down** *the* **saints** of the Highest One, and he will intend to make alterations in times and in law" (Daniel 7:25).

What's also important to note is that my son and soon to be new daughter were watching the entire scene take place. So, while sharing the details with them, I am always quick to boast about my weakness of not being able to believe and ask for the additional fee to be *eliminated*—but only **reduced**. But this has proved to be a blessing since God always, and will forever cause all things to work out for good! And may I say, I am determined to not be in this place again!

As I said earlier, I really need to create one document in order for me to easily search through, and I'd like to encourage you to do the same thing. All of us need to equip ourselves and arm ourselves with testimonies that are at our fingertips when the enemy strikes out against our faith. Sometimes the Lord is moving so quickly in my life, I barely have time to sit down and write down what has happened in one day! However, I will simply trust the Lord to help me get these testimonies written down, then I hope to also sow them into the lives of others and submit all of them to the RMI website.

What about you? How will you fare during a crisis? Every day, or at least once a week, be sure to gather the testimonies from the RMI website, then make sure they are easily found and searchable. Also be certain you have your own testimonies to share—begin to expect trials, look forward to them, and flourish because of them! I promise that if you sow what you have into the lives of others, encouragement—you will see your own faith and also your blessings grow!!

If the testimonies in this book have helped build your faith, then copy the parts you want to save. Consider having different sections, such as your personal or favorite financial testimonies to read yourself and share with others. Soon you'll be submitting more praises of how the Lord has blessed you financially like He's done for me. And whether you're limited to a reduction or elimination, be sure you always are equally excited to boast about your weaknesses. Keep it real so others can relate.

Lastly, be sure you do the same thing by posting your relationship testimonies, and maybe even another section with the testimonies for a physical healing! Together, as encouraging women, we will WOW the world with what God can do—the impossible!! And how having Him as a Husband means being carried over the threshold of difficulties!!!

Chapter 8

Embracing the Poverty

"Blessed are the **poor** in **spirit**,
for theirs is the kingdom of heaven."
—Matthew 5:3

Embracing the poverty—what does that mean? Does it only refer to money, like our finances? Or is this a principle or idea that transcends every area of our lives—*embracing* rather than *running* from lack?

In His Beatitudes Jesus said that those who lacked, like the poor, are those who are blessed—do you and I honestly believe that? We say we do, but very few of us come to that place of choosing to *embrace* this principle, so because it's more acceptable, we choose, instead, to embrace the mindset of this world.

Let's face it, it's difficult for us to watch the "wicked" increase and prosper while at the same time we (who do all we can to serve and love the Lord as His bride in our hearts and actions)—sit in need and lack. This is when we have to decide if what we do is based and has its foundation on doing what's right for the sake of right, or doing what is right for the sake of gain.

Recently my children have also been struggling silently with this entire concept. Their father left our family in pursuit of sin—adultery once again. And since then they have had a front row seat watching their father continuing to "seemingly" prosper while we are currently struggling in very deep and dangerous lack. With tears, just the other day, my teenage daughter asked why it seems that God is blessing her dad for doing what was wrong, and at the same time punishing us for doing what was right.

It often does seem like we are being punished, not just to we who are living through it, but to those who are watching our lives. Is God punishing us? I remember vividly living through these feelings several years ago. It was I who was in tears, lying on top of my bed holding my little six-year-old son (who's now an adult) and he was crying, which is why I began to cry. Very much like Erin shares in one of her books, while I was doing everything I could to do what was right, for the sake of my children, I had just heard that his daddy, my husband, had taken the other woman on a trip to meet his family. Even worse, I also heard that his family had embraced his new relationship and the first OW (other woman) into their family. My six-year-old, however, didn't know why his daddy was visiting family (or who he had taken with him), all he knew was that he had taken a trip and left him behind. Poor dear.

It is so vivid in my mind how much of a catalyst this trip was to what changed everything (though I didn't know it at the time). It was the beginning of the end for this ungodly relationship and for my marriage to be restored (which also meant my son's daddy moving back home). Nevertheless, this event caused everything in my life to begin racing downhill. I don't remember all of the details, but one-by-one my world began crashing down around me. I do remember my husband coming to visit me one day. We were separated (he'd left and was living with the first other woman), and he stood there telling me quite clearly that if this is the way God rewarded good people (referring to what was happening in my life), then why do what was right?

After he walked out of my darkened room, it was then I had to make a choice, and my choice was to *embrace* the poverty and lack for the sake of doing what was right. No matter what, I had to do what was right, what He said, and He said, "Blessed are the poor in spirit." In the end, I was blessed and because of me choosing a path that was difficult (even crazy), and a life that those closest to me mocked, He blessed me and my children. We came through everything with a testimony that has helped encourage more people than I could count.

Questions not Easy to Answer

It was just last night that I once again found myself sitting with my other daughter who was facing the same questions as her brother had asked, "Why are we doing what is right when it seems as if it does no good, and that the opposite, doing what is wrong, achieves the real rewards?" Time and again she had opened her heart to her father, while he hurt and rejected her. Birthdays are always a time of vulnerability, and she had just been horribly hurt. In addition, she had been through quite a lot besides things with her father.

Right then I had to make my choice, once again, to choose to *embrace* the poverty, even if it was only for the sake of doing what was right for the sake of doing right, because there was no way I wanted to envy wickedness. I chose, again, to embrace poverty— pulling it close to my heart. How was I going to answer my children's questions?

In doing what was right, by pulling the poverty close to my heart rather than rejecting it (as any mother may feel like doing), *immediately* my eyes saw everything in a totally new light! Even though my ex-husband (my daughters' father) seems to "have it all"—financial security that our family now lacked, we had much, much, much more than money could ever buy. First, I told her, "I have you! I have your love, and the joy of being here with you, to comfort you. And it's just not you who I have, or you having me. We have … [and I began to name each of her siblings]." Instantly, almost on cue, we heard the other children in the other room who were still at the dinner table, laughing and talking. It was then that we both realized, at that moment, that we were the ones who were rich—because we each had Him—as a loving Father and a new faithful Husband!

Even if we lost our home, lost our entire income, lost our reputation, and every other physical security, it would never compare to what we had, and had gained, by embracing God's choice for us— going through our situation of facing poverty. By facing the poverty, then choosing to embrace it, we found ourselves rich! We had discovered that the real wealth is not in what we thought we needed, but what is really important.

Dear one, if you are in a similar situation: you are looking intently at the poverty or lack that is before you with fear and trepidation—I understand. Right now, you may see that there is no way out if you move forward, and turning back looks so tempting. But let me encourage you to *embrace* your poverty no matter how terrifying it may seem. For as soon as you do, you will find, as I did, that the darkness it not at all terrifying like you once feared. As soon as you choose to embrace it, rather than run from it, I promise a small light will appear. And His light will be a beam allowing you to immediately see the truth clearly.

Don't run from poverty and lack—I promise that you don't want to miss what is up ahead by turning back now!

Also, precious one. If you have lost your family and everyone who you loved and who once loved you, please be sure you read the first two books in this series: *Finding the Abundant Life* and *Living the Abundant Life*. When you have His love, and His presence, I can assure you that your life will never feel empty and you'll never ever feel alone ever again.

My Eighth of Many Financial Testimonies

"Fit for a Queen"

Let me tell you that once you get a hold of the *power of giving*, you just get so excited to see where your next opportunity lies! The sweetest opportunity to give out of my lack, thus far, occurred on my daughter's 15th birthday—her heavenly Father chose to bless her socks off!!

Honestly I am not sure how it all came about, but it has been the desires of my heart since moving into our new home (before my husband left) to replace each of our old bunk beds, each with queen size beds. My reason is that they are large enough for a married couple to sleep on, and are also good for sleepovers. A king size is too large for most rooms, and the queen size sheets and comforters seem to be the size that I frequently find on sale.

So in moving the rooms around when my son left, my daughter was getting her own room for the first time in her life, and I just knew that her Father was about to bless her tremendously. I had watched how she handled and blessed her cousin who lived with us for a year: always giving, apologizing for everything that went wrong and taking the full blame or responsibility even though she was younger and normally nothing was *her* fault. My daughter said she wanted to because she said, "I have been a Christian much longer Mom." [My niece had asked about many things when she lived with us, and as a result accepted the Lord—the first in her family to become a Believer!]

My daughter has not only given to her cousin, but she has looked for opportunities to bless others, it seems like thousands of times over the past two years. Prior to focusing on her cousin, she had been concentrating on giving to her older sister, since her older sister had been going through a very tough time with what happened with her dad. So, just like with her cousin, even though she was younger, when anything happened with her older sister, she took and continues to take full responsibility when something negative happens, which is undoubtedly due to her heart and passion for the Lord. Time and again I told her that she couldn't give like that without her Father blessing her double (and with a good attitude ten times over), each time I saw she was again giving to others.

God chose her birthday to bless her—He showed up right in the midst of another trial, which is so like a loving Father would!

The day her dad was coming to get her to take her away from home for a two-week visit with him and the woman he was living with (something that she was really struggling with, but had surrendered to the Lord), she and I went out looking for a bed for her. We seemed to go everywhere, but nothing was falling into place. After many stops, I sat there in the car and told her that I didn't want to force a blessing, and when it is from the Lord things just fall into place and He blesses us beyond words. Bless her heart, she agreed and said she could wait. That's when the blessing immediately began to materialize!

While driving home I turned onto a side street to avoid traffic, and spotted a warehouse furniture store. I found out later that the owners and manager are close friends of my son's fiancé's parents. When the manager asked if he could help, I told him exactly what I wanted to pay for a pillow-top mattress and box spring—and he sold it to me for the price I quoted! Let me tell you that that the price I said I wanted to pay and what I paid for it was ridiculous! I couldn't believe that I said what I said. But, immediately, I knew my Husband was about to do something wonderfully loving!!

Next, I asked if he had a headboard and he pointed to two. My daughter was drawn to the darker one, and then the man suddenly said he remembered something, and led us to a backroom, pointing to the headboard of her dreams!! She said it was *exactly* what she had always wanted! When I asked the price, he *gave* it to me for nothing!!

The next day after we celebrated her birthday and we even splurged and had lunch out, we all headed back to our home, but a few of us had a couple of errands to run. I had no idea where I was going, or why, but the Lord led me to a store where He first reminded me that I promised to pick up something for my son (isn't HE just so good??). While there, while talking on my cell phone, I found myself standing in front of the most gorgeous comforter set!! It had decorative pillows similar to what we had looked at the day before.

My son and his fiancé (who are both known for their good taste and impeccable style) just "happened to be" in the same store, so to be sure that these were, in fact, "in style" I headed toward where they said they were. As soon as I turned the corner, my son's fiancé was in awe at how gorgeous the comforter set was while my daughter could hear her say how gorgeous it was (since she was on the phone with me). My daughter said she just asked her dad if he would buy a comforter for her, and he said, yes, but adding it was way more than he gave for birthdays. So seeing the opportunity, I said whatever he didn't pay, I would. When her dad heard that, he said he would pay it all!! Oh, the joy of being married to my Husband whose resources are endless!!

Remember, whenever there is injustice, God promises double. Divorce is an injustice to the children, so I always tell my children to **anticipate *double* rather than worry about the *apparent* destruction.

During the two weeks that my younger children were visiting their dad, the older children painted my daughter's bedroom room, and her bathroom! After her bedroom was dry, my sons moved the new furniture in. Then the Lord orchestrated new curtains, sheets, comforter, pillows, and even a new dresser *through* the gifts of other family members along with added money from her savings account for babysitting. In about eight hours, this precious girl who has been through so so much, and who did it with such a tender heart, is going to walk into a new bedroom that you would see on a television designer show. It's honestly beyond anything that I have ever seen in a magazine—and it is all for her!

Her Father wants her to remember each night when she goes to bed and each morning when she wakes up, just how much He loves her, protects her, and cherishes her—in her new room—now, fit for a queen.

Chapter 9

God's Waiting Room

"They that wait upon the Lord,
will renew their strength…"
—Isaiah 40:31

Sitting here in the middle of the night, listening to the rain outside and the stillness inside, I realized that I am in God's waiting room.

You and I have been here millions of times, and if you are like me, you thought you had learned how to endure the wait. Sleep is a good way to pass the time, but then when awakened, your mind begins to think, to plan, to wonder, to think, and think some more.

Getting up meant only thinking some more, so I began to busy myself. You've been there too, I know I am not alone, but we feel we are alone don't we?

Yes, of course we pray, and as His bride we talk to our Husband—doing our best to listen, but we only hear the rain and our own thoughts. In God's waiting room, He often chooses to remain silent, except for the few encouraging words that we hear, you know, like the verses that explain just why we must wait—like our opening verse: we wait so that our strength can be renewed. If that's true why do we often feel weaker?

After reading quite a few devotionals online, I sat here wondering if I could possibly go back to sleep, and if that hot milk I drank would help. For a split second, I thought of turning on the television, but that's not at all *spiritual*—I need to do something much more productive! That's when my compassionate Husband put a thought in my mind that had to be Him. It was a revelation that rang so true, and its principle encompassed everything that you and I are experiencing right now.

What you and I are doing in God's waiting room is only going to help pass the "time"—it's simply a means to occupy *our* time so that the wait doesn't feel as long. What you and I do during the wait will have *nothing* at all to do with making the wait shorter—there is simply an "appointed time." It will also have nothing at all to do with making that "thing" we are waiting for any grander, or more magnificent. Just like every blessing that is bestowed on you and me, it's all from Him— we didn't earn it nor do we deserve it, and we are foolish if we think that we do or did. It's what He longs to give us because we are His bride.

What is it that you are waiting for dear friend and fellow bride? Again, if you are like me it is not just one thing, it is dozens of things: health issues, money issues, ministry issues, relationship issues— and let me not forget to mention—each one *appearing* hopeless. Well, of course, isn't that why we are here in God's waiting room? Are we so foolish that we have forgotten that apart from Him we can do nothing? And isn't every good gift from above?

So why bother doing anything? Why will you and I bother getting up in the morning and starting a new day, doing the same things, working just as diligently when we know that it will do little to no good to get that appointment with our miracle?

Right before I picked up my computer to get these thoughts on paper, I pictured myself in one of those doctor's waiting rooms filled with: magazines, people, and closed doors surrounded me. We try to read one of those magazines, but our mind is inside those doors, behind that frosted glass. One by one someone else's name is called—while we wait.

However, this is not an accurate picture and as I realized it, I had to make the proper adjustments to what I was envisioning. You see, in my mind I have made a set appointment. I may have to wait longer than expected, for some odd reason offices seem to schedule too many patients/clients for the time allotted, but nevertheless, at some point in time, on that day, my name *will* be called. You see—what I've been envisioning isn't accurate due to one major flaw.

We don't know *exactly* when our appointment is, do we? We each *hope* and pray that our appointment is for today: our miracle, our breakthrough, our situation will change—today—but, alas, tomorrow comes and we often find we are still waiting.

So I let my mind, instead, imagine waiting in some foreign country where there is no guarantee that you or I will be seen, ever. You and I are more like a humble soul who travels by foot where the rumors are told of a missionary who's come with medicine. So we get there with the great masses of sick and dying, hoping that help will make it through the crowd to find us. There is no appointment, and no need to complain to anyone. Our only hope is to wait, and hope—hoping that we will be seen, and that miraculously we might be helped due to our traveling the distance.

Yes, that describes our situation a bit better, doesn't it? We simply hope, pray, and hang on to the faith that says that we **did** hear from God and that His promises *were* for us. Nevertheless, doubt often creeps in to taunt us, especially when we think of or witness first hand, all those "others" who'd waited, but then for some reason, walked out of God's waiting room. Why'd they go? Was it because they were too tired to wait or did they realize that God had another plan and they were waiting in the wrong room: the wrong miracle, or wrong prayer, maybe they had the wrong motive for waiting?

Certainly, I can throw out many questions, but where are the answers you ask? Who's got the answers anyway—clearly not me. Understanding this wait only makes sense when I look back at what God has already done in my life and in your life; only by looking **at what He's done** can any of this chaos make sense.

It's His timing I am talking about.

When I look back at so many times I have waited, I was waiting so that each situation was perfectly set in place. The home that I now live in sat unoccupied for *over a year* while we waited for *over a year* to sell our previous house. Why? Well, just one reason was the price. Our builder chose to sell it to us **at his cost**— just barely breaking even, certainly something he wouldn't have done had he not had to wait to sell it. Had we not waited to sell our previous house.

Then rewinding to us buying our previous home before the last. That house never even went on the market. When the sellers found themselves with two homes for *more than a year,* it was then that they decided they had to sell off hundreds of surrounding acres, reduce the price to a ridiculous amount, and only then we were called out of our "waiting room" a very tiny little rental we thought we might live in **forever** (planning we'd stay just a month or two).

May I also explain that each time we were asked to "wait" it ultimately made our miracle all the sweeter—it was never just about the price we inevitably paid for each (far below what anyone could imagine). No, it was because it made all of us appreciate what He'd done that much more and, for me personally, because it helped me understand. My wait helped me empathize and inevitably be prepared to encourage others who must wait, encouraging them with compassion.

Each and every time we wait will have its own unique purpose, but only when we take the time to look back and see what He's done. And isn't that what we have now—time—lots of time?

So rather than just trying to busy ourselves with magazines, or television, or even good works that we hope will amount to something, and get us out of God's waiting room sooner, I think that looking back at the purpose and perfect plan of previous waiting rooms will prove to be the best method for not just enduring the wait, but *enjoying* God's waiting room.

Enjoy the wait.

My Ninth of Many Financial Testimonies

"Anniversary Vacation"

When I got to the end of this chapter I had to stop and think of a financial testimony to write. God does so many things in my life, some big and some small, but with all the amazing ones that I have written so far, I knew I needed a big one to share!

So I stopped writing and asked the Lord to remind me of yet another a financial blessing that has happened that I must have forgotten about, and that's just what He did. While talking to my daughter on the phone, I mentioned the dates that I would be gone to which she replied, "Oh, are you *really* going?" While excitedly sharing all the details to what God had done, I realized He had also reminded me of something incredible that He'd also blessed me with!!

The blessing began right after I found the honeymoon trip to Hawaii that I spoke about in chapter 5 "Hopelessly in Need of Him". That trip had used up only 3000 points but another 2000, would expire by May 31st. Honestly, I hadn't wanted to go anywhere else after all the traveling I had done over the previous two years, and therefore, at one point, I offered these points to my ex-husband as a blessing. By following the principle in Matthew 5:39-42 of blessing your enemies (when he forcibly took the children to his home when he had promised he would only take them if they *wanted* to go) is what always takes the sting out of any injustice. Yet, he had refused the blessing of the points, so I'd sought the Lord again about the points that needed to be used. By the way, if you give and it's not accepted, has no effect on you being blessed—isn't He just too amazingly wonderful?

With the points I had left, He reminded me of us visiting a quaint little town in the South. Another reason He reminded me of, was that it was something my children had spoken about fairly often—they missed eating at a southern barbeque restaurant that has been our family's favorite for years. Immediately, their Father and my Husband, in one single stroke, pulled it all together one morning a few weeks ago for us to go! There are so many exciting details about what He'd done, but let me highlight just a few of my favorites:

First, while visiting there, we wanted to go to a popular amusement park again. We'd gone there as a family and it had left fond memories for our children. That's when He reminded me about the VIP passes but they (weren't) were no longer valid. Nevertheless, I called and was told that we could get in for half price. Even though I know contentment is what we should have, I was simply led to not "settle" for less than free, so I told my children, "You'll see, we'll get in for free. I am not sure how, but how is not my problem, it's His. And nothing is a problem for my Husband and your Father!"

Two weeks later I opened a letter that included *new* VIP passes!

And when my daughter opened the letter and began reading, it said, in black and white, that the pass not only gave us FREE admission to the amusement park (in we'd hope to go to), but it went onto say that we'd get some sort of discount to a dinner show where my children have always wanted to go to!! Amazingly awesome, right?!?!

Dear bride, each of us will receive double when we simply look for it and trust that as His bride, and as your children's Father, amazingly wonderful experiences are in store for us! There's nothing special about me, He cares for you just as much—simply begin to sense His love surrounding you and return that love that He longs for. Keep Him first in your heart, and you'll see you and your children blessed. But, yearning for another, and you'll soon see your life and your children's life taking on second best too.

The second part, as I mentioned above, our family loves southern food. Once the dates were booked, I went online to see if our favorite southern barbeque restaurant was anywhere close to where we were going. Would you believe that there is one right on our way? Of course, you would since you, as His bride, see things differently! This means we will be able to eat barbeque on our first night and again in the afternoon we leave. Nothing could be as perfect even if I had tried, but it simply fell into place with no effort or thought on my part! Double blessings are His specialty.

Lastly, my favorite blessing is when I was booking our reservations. I'd asked for the dates that I wanted to go to but there were no vacancies, so rather than think I missed what He'd led me to do, I asked what dates *were* available—then readily *agreed* to those dates. Are you ready? Just two days ago I realized what dates those were.

You may know my testimony well enough, about how my husband walked in one day and announced he was divorcing me and even though (at the time) it *appeared* to be a horrible and frightening experience, it had turned out to be one of the greatest blessings of my life. So much so, that I decided to celebrate that special day each year!

I suppose I don't need to tell you what day the vacation begins on do I? Yes! We begin our vacation on my anniversary. Then, just to make sure that I knew without a doubt it was for that reason, our vacation is beginning on an unusual day, on a Tuesday of all days, on the *exact* anniversary of the day my earthly husband walked out, officially making me HIS bride!!!

──────── Chapter 10 ────────

Don't Settle for Less

"O LORD, we have **waited** for You eagerly;
Your name, even Your memory,
is the desire of our souls."
—Isaiah 26:8

Have you ever waited for God to show up, but when He did you refused the package? You may not have done it intentionally, but what I have recently noticed is that when our miracle comes by way of the wrong person or arrives in the midst of the wrong circumstance, we refuse the miracle and unknowingly settle for less. We simply want to choose the "blessings" of our own making, the things we believe we have earned. How horribly sad.

To help you fully understand what I mean, below are two heartbreaking stories in the Bible where, without knowing it, the recipient settled for less. Both were part of Elisha's amazing ministry. The first involves the king of Israel and the second, the widow and the oil (a story you may already know).

"When Elisha became sick with the illness of which he was to die, Joash the king of Israel came down to him and wept over him and said, 'My father, my father, the chariots of Israel and its horsemen!'

"Elisha said to him, 'Take a bow and arrows.' So he took a bow and arrows. Then he said to the king of Israel, 'Put your hand on the bow.' And he put his hand on it, then Elisha laid his hands on the king's hands.

"He said, 'Open the window toward the east,' and he opened it. Then Elisha said, 'Shoot!' And he shot. And he said, "The LORD'S arrow of victory, even the arrow of victory over Aram; for you will defeat the Arameans at Aphek until you have destroyed them.'

"Then he said, 'Take the arrows,' and he took them. And he said to the king of Israel, 'Strike the ground,' and he struck it *three times and stopped.*

"So the man of God was *angry* with him and said, 'You should have struck five or six times, then you would have struck Aram until you would have destroyed it. But now you shall strike Aram only three times'" (2 Kings 13:14–19). Next is the widow...

"Now a certain woman of the wives of the sons of the prophets cried out to Elisha, 'Your servant my husband is dead, and you know that your servant feared the LORD; and the creditor has come to take my two children to be his slaves.'

"Elisha said to her, 'What shall I do for you? Tell me, what do you have in the house?' And she said, 'Your maidservant has nothing in the house except a jar of oil.'

"Then he said, 'Go, borrow vessels at large for yourself from all your neighbors, even empty vessels; **do not get a** *few.* And you shall go in and shut the door behind you and your sons, and pour out into all these vessels, and you shall set aside what is full.'

"So she went from him and shut the door behind her and her sons; they were bringing the vessels to her and she poured. When the vessels were full, she said to her son, 'Bring me another vessel.' And he said to her, 'There is not one vessel more.' **And the oil stopped.**

"Then she came and told the man of God. And he said, 'Go, sell the oil and pay your debt, and you and your sons can live on the rest'" (2 Kings 4:1-10).

These are the stories that came to mind just recently when "settling for less" happened to my precious daughter. It caught my attention to this all-important principle when we foolishly and often ignorantly *choose* to settle for less.

For several months my daughter has put away every penny of her income with the desire to buy herself a car. She apologizes almost every morning for me having to drive her for work, even though I tell her each time that I am already up, and that I thoroughly enjoy the time I have alone with her. Still, she apologizes.

When she reached her goal of how much she'd hoped to put down on a car, she began asking guys she knew to help her find a good car. When she told me, the first thing I thought of was how would her brothers feel when they heard that she asked a guy friend rather than asking them? Then I thought of how our Husband feels when we ask one of our friends rather than asking our best Friend who never will leave us or forsake us.

The principle of seeking others rather than our Husband took on an entirely new level when week after week my daughter was sad and disappointed because her dad was not helping her buy that perfect car she found and also because she wanted **him** to co-sign for the loan. I sat listening each time she told me until the day she finally asked me what to do. That's when I could finally share my heart with her, explaining how often we look to others rather than looking to her true Father for every need she has.

It took some time but I finally convinced my daughter to look to her Father for her car. As soon as she did, it took less than two hours to discover that our neighbor found all their gorgeous cars at an auction, and that the following week our neighbors said they could get her one at a dealer's price. Then the Lord led me to, once again, offer to co-sign for her. Very soon the car, which was *beyond* her dreams, would be hers!

Yet somewhere in the midst of waiting, she reverted back. Isn't that just like all of us? We are so accustomed to the ways of relying on and trusting others, and ourselves, that we are caught in the habit. That's why He lovingly surrounds us with fellow believers who will encourage us and remind us to trust Him alone, which happened with my daughter. So, again, very soon, she was relying on her Father and speaking positively about what He was about to do.

That's when something unexpected happened. While filling out the loan papers something caught my eye, something was written at the top, when, in an instant, this verse came to mind: "I have been young and now I am old, yet I have not seen the righteous forsaken or his descendants begging bread" (Psalm 37:25). All I could imagine was what the Psalmist would do if he saw me today. No, I was not begging for "bread" but here I was begging a credit union for a loan. My heart grieved when I thought, again, how my Husband was feeling by going to someone other than Him.

Had I asked my Husband for the money to buy a car for our daughter? No, instead I'd gone off to seek help from someone else! So how could I look at anyone else, like my daughter for instance, when I was doing the very same thing, only more severely, since I'm His bride, traveling along my journey with my Love.

Yet, rather than feeling like I'd messed up, believing the lie, which comes with guilt, that this meant that I would have to forgo the blessing. Instead, I have come to understand more fully His incredible forgiving love and His immeasurable grace that sets us free from worry, doubt and fear. "There is no fear in love; but **perfect love** *casts out fear...*" (1 John 4:18). Oh, His love!!

Because even when we fail, as I knew I had, He is right there next to us, ready and excited to bless us! Isn't that what this verse means? "And we know that God causes **all** *things to work together for* **good** to those who love God, to those who are called according to His purpose" (Romans 8:28).

So rather than worry, or fret, I turned my face up to Him, tearfully trusting to find His blessing in this mistake and shortcoming of mine. Immediately and amazingly—I discovered the most incredible blessing I could never have imagined!

The discovery began with a tremendous trial as most blessings begin. It was just a little over a year ago when I got a call that the refinancing on my house came to a sudden halt with some shocking news. It was during the divorce process, when, unbeknownst to me, my ex-husband's attorney had placed a huge financial judgment against me in order for his client, my ex, to be assured that he would get his portion of the equity in our home.

It wasn't until just a few weeks ago that I understood the second stipulation of this—my ex-husband was *sure* that I would lose my home. He had witnessed my "spiritual weirdness" as he referred to it since I have been a zealot for a very long time. This led to him taking drastic measures.

So, does this mean that you and I are destined to experience "lack" due to the actions of others? Actually the opposite will happen as long as we are trusting Him. And our blessings will be *due* to that evil (that we must refuse to resist) with will catapult us to greatness. "But I say to you, do *not* resist an evil person; but whoever slaps you on your right cheek, turn the other to him also. If anyone wants to sue you and take your shirt, let him have your coat also. Whoever forces you to go one mile, go with him two" (Matthew 5:38–40). Not resisting evil, will also gain the attention of others. He does this to give us a testimony to share with others— in order for the hurting and suffering souls to experience His love!!

The day I found out that my credit was ruined (a judgment is like a bankruptcy only it lasts for 10 years not 7), I blurted out something, while laughing, that caught my attention when I said it. I said, *"Well, that must mean that I won't* need *credit—I'll be buying everything for cash!"* In my mind, I envisioned buying larger items, such as cars or even houses for cash. Though it seemed far beyond my faith, I couldn't help but hold this thought up and compare it with God's ability, which simply meant—nothing, not one thing, is impossible with God!

The day the verse about "begging bread" jumped into view, I also caught a glimpse of what my Husband might do next. And, this same vision flew across my mind not just once, but it happened twice more that same day. The next morning the same thing happened, until I followed that vision and went into my online bank account.

What's crazy is that for week's money had been "piling up" in my account and each time I saw it, I kept asking my Husband what He wanted me to do with it. Because I still have mounds of debt, I instinctively thought, pay down the debt. But each time I asked He told me, no, that debt is His, that He (like my sins) had been paid for. So, since all my bills were being paid on time, nothing was late, I again asked Him what the accumulated cash was for? That day my eyes were open when He said, "Look, there's *more than enough* to pay **cash** for our daughter's car"!!

The instant I saw it, my daughter walked into the room, almost on cue. When I asked her to sit down, and fully explained the plan, she sat there stunned. Nevertheless, she quickly explained how much she could pay me back each month, which allowed me to explain to her that just as in salvation, God never asks us to pay Him back. The truth is, we can't, and even if we could, He doesn't want our money or our works or anything but our love for Him. He wants us to appreciate and experience His goodness, His love! That morning I wanted my daughter to experience firsthand the goodness, awesomeness, and faithfulness of the One who I had fallen madly and passionately in love with again and again and again.

Yet, before we could move forward, with a few days before the auction, I could bask in His love—knowing that I would be able to write out a check, *me,* for the amount to purchase our daughter a car for cash. No loans, no need to borrow any more, not ever. I was so excited that I found myself sharing this with each of my children, and a few of my friends I ran into. By the way, do you remember my telling you that you should be careful **never** to share what He shows you to do until *after* you do it, because the enemy will try to stop it from happening? Well, with all my heart I wish I had remembered. Not for my sake, but for my daughter's.

By the time the auction came around, my daughter had refused to take my money. One of her siblings had convinced her that I "couldn't afford it," and she had no right take advantage of me and that she should instead go to her dad. By the time we spoke, my daughter had already turned back to looking to her dad for him to co-sign on a loan. She decided to settle for less.

I knew to try to convince her would be wrong, I know her well enough to know that she would resist my efforts besides, as a mother, we are to live our faith in love and share when we are asked—not push our beliefs on anyone.

When my daughter, once again, began pursuing, hoping and praying for her dad to co-sign and get her a car, God gave her what she asked for. She was excited when she told me that his new wife brought up the subject, and excited when they, finally, took her out to find her a car. Sadly, instead of finding her dream car, her father and wife told her, it wasn't sensible enough. In addition, they lingered long into the night telling everyone that was there that night that if she bought her dream car, she wouldn't be able to *afford* new tires if she needed them, she couldn't *afford* the repairs if something went wrong, and on and on they went.

The night this conversation took place, my daughter was not there. I alone listened as her dad and stepmom told everyone about the car that she *needed* was the one "they" got for her, "It's a sensible car, the make, and model that her grandmother(drove). Even though it was priced the same as the 'dream' car she wanted (then both laughed), who did she think she was to even *want* a car like that?!?" they went onto say. My heart grieved.

There have been so many horrendous trials with this car that seemed to happen almost everyday—yet my daughter is determined to prove to me it was the car that she was supposed to get.

Yet I know in my heart how her Father's blessings are designed to grab the attention of everyone—especially us. I know how my heart sings each time I get in and drive my car, the car my Husband gave me. I feel so loved and yes, sometimes even undeserved, because what I drive is a miracle of the most amazing kind. I wanted a blessing like that for my daughter too, but sadly, she settled for less.

My Tenth of Many Financial Testimonies

"By Your Words"

At the same time, the above was happening to my daughter, her brother was going through a similar situation of settling for less, rather than following the blessing his Father had for him.

Because my son has his own business, there are often lean times, times when he looked as if he would come up short, but each time, of course (since he is a giver of the most amazing kind) he always paid his bills and had enough for his needs.

Then one morning he told me that he was going to go out and get a part-time job just so he never needed to worry about paying his bills. He wanted "just enough" to make his car payment, insurance, gas, etc., he said. Within a week he had an amazing job offer to waiter where he would get great tips. Yet, night after night he came home exhausted and disappointed with the small number of tips he was making.

Since I was the one who saw the sign for this job and encouraged him to take it, I felt responsible and spoke to my Husband about it. That's when He lovingly replayed what my son had said, he said he wanted to make "just enough" to pay his bills, and God had answered his prayers accordingly.

When I realized what had happened, I share this revelation with my son. At first, I think he was thinking I was being a bit too spiritually weird, but he couldn't shake the thought that I could actually be right. It didn't take too many long days at his business, then leaving to work nights for him to change his plea to his Father— asking Him to send him more business, and to bless him with abundance!

His Father chose to bless him while we were having breakfast with his dad— he got the call that left him speechless. A guy he'd met only once had taken notice of him for his outstanding work, explaining that he was pulling a team together and wanted him for the position. Then he said what the pay rate would be—my son could *not* believe it—the pay was what he would make if he worked 10 days as a waiter with great tips! In addition, the guy said this would not be a one-time deal, this additional business would be ongoing (however, the thief almost stole it from him; the details will be in the next chapter).

My son immediately let go of being a waiter and trying to earn just enough. And the more he looks to his Father the more the blessings are flowing into his life. More and more calls are coming into his business—more than he said he ever believed he would ever have! It has even spilled over to his brother who is getting married and was hoping for some side jobs to earn more money!

Following the same principle, looking to his Father, my son was also hired for the same project and there are many more projects up ahead for them both. Now, due to what he continues to witness his brother does, he too is trying to bring himself to trust the Lord totally rather than relying on a steady paycheck where he works now and hopes to venture out on his own. To be continued as the blessings unfold...

Chapter 11

Shake it Off

"But Paul shook the snake off into the fire
and suffered no ill effects"
—Acts 28:5

Soon after the Apostle Paul was shipwrecked, it says that "Paul gathered a pile of brushwood and, as he put it on the fire, a viper, driven out by the heat, fastened itself on his hand. When the islanders saw the snake hanging from his hand, they said to each other, 'This man must be a murderer; for though he escaped from the sea, justice has not allowed him to live.' But Paul *shook the snake off into the fire and suffered no ill effects.* The people expected him to swell up or suddenly fall dead, but after waiting a long time and seeing nothing unusual happen to him, they changed their minds and said he was a god" (Acts 28:3–6).

This is a great story of the Bible that has so much meaning. In this chapter, I hope to use this as a picture to understand the principle of how we must act when something comes in to kill our miracle.

We all know that the "The *thief* comes only to **steal** and **kill** and **destroy**; I [Jesus] came that they may have life, and have it abundantly" (John 10:10). Since we can be easy prey to the enemy and his schemes, we often miss out on abundance when we are not wise. "I am sending you like lambs into a pack of wolves. So be as *wise* as snakes and as *innocent* as doves" (Matthew 10:16). We need to heed the warning as the Message Bible says, "Stay alert. This is hazardous work I'm assigning you. You're going to be like sheep running through a wolf pack, so don't call attention to yourselves. Be as cunning as a snake, inoffensive as a dove."

The best way for me to help you to understand, and then to apply this principle, is to share with you a few short testimonies. The first involves my son's soon-to-be mother-in-law.

Just before the wedding shower that she and I were organizing, while bending over to empty her dishwasher, she pulled her back out. When I heard what happened, I immediately spoke to my Husband (remember, He's also the Physician), asking Him to heal her. Each day I heard that she was "trusting the Lord" for her recovery. Then while she was praying, she sensed she should visit my chiropractor, who her daughter had been seeing— who just happens to be an awesome young Christian, who speaks often about God's ability to heal us.

A few days later, there she was up and walking around, slowly, but walking. No matter how many people encouraged her to go to the doctor (even the chiropractor said it was serious and she should go), she just kept saying that she *knew* that God would heal her. Let me stop here and tell you that none of us is against doctors. Nevertheless, all of us (in the testimony) believe that we need to seek the Lord, our Physician, allowing Him to lead us to know what to do. It's when we "put our faith in our doctor" and run to him or her, that we are doomed. No one can be first in our lives—God says to put Him first and as His bride how could we dare trust anyone else!

The day before the wedding shower we were at her house for a meeting with a wedding coordinator. A few minutes before she arrived, a close friend of both of ours showed up. The conversation turned to how she'd thrown *her* back out but God was healing her, to which our friend was quick to say, "You're gonna need surgery! I know, I have the same thing. No chiropractor's gonna help. Nope, you're gonna need surgery!" Wow, talk about fear getting a hold of you!! Just like that viper—it jumped on her, yet THANK YOU, my DARLING—she shook it off!!

My son's soon-to-be mother-in-law said, kindly, but convincingly, "But I am already healing and so much better!! On Monday I couldn't walk, then each day I got better and better…see?" as she got up and walked across the room. Had she agreed with the lie, and began to allow that viper fear to get a hold of her, I believe she would have been headed for surgery. Instead, she is now, just weeks later, walking around perfectly healed and completely whole!

Now, another example was my son. In the last chapter I told you how a viper tried to come take hold of my son's miracle (when my son began trusting His Father and get ongoing business) but I said that I would share the details with you in this chapter.

My son had already begun to benefit from the newly formed team by working a couple of days, but then on the first day they called to apologize saying they only had a lesser position open, but my son rejoiced, and excitedly said, "Hey, that's fine." When he told me about it, I told him he would be blessed for having the right heart and positive response since it proved he continued to trust his Father.

Mothers, can I stop for a moment and share something with you? Do you know that when you speak you can speak *blessings* into your children's lives? It is so true, the principle says, "With the fruit of a man's mouth his stomach will be satisfied; He will be satisfied with the product of his lips. *Death and life* are in the power of the tongue, and those who love it will eat its fruit" (Proverbs 18:20-22). "One who **guards** his mouth *preserves his life*; one who **opens it** *comes to ruin"* (Proverbs 13:3). I know that I will write more about this in the sequel to this book that I am excited to begin that I am entitling, *Moving Mountains*, but for right now, simply pay close attention to *what* you say, making sure it's positive. However, you will probably find, as I did, that it is always easier to see something in someone else rather than seeing a fault in ourselves. So watch what other people around you say (good and faithful statements versus dread and fearful statements) and what happens as a result. Now back to my story…

When my son got home that evening he told me excitedly that when he got to the job, after excitedly accepting the lesser position, they told him that a key position just opened up, but he would only get the lower pay rate. Again he told me he was really excited to accept the position, which resulted in them being blown away by his God-given, heavily volunteered, abilities and talents. Yahoo! "I have **no greater joy** than this, to hear of my children walking in the truth" (3 John 1:4). Due to his positive acceptance at each turn, the very next day they told him he'd would be paid the higher rate with the higher position, which he praised God openly for that led to a surprise—an extra day of work that no one else got!

The blessings continued the following week, when he had another high paying job lined up and was enthusiastically sharing his testimony to anyone and everyone—telling everyone of how he was trusting his Father for work. So of course, the viper jumped out of the fire again when he got a call from his close friend who was also part of the upcoming team for the following week and explained that the entire plan for the team, he said, was "just not going to work out" and would be dissolving.

When I came out for breakfast my son told me "the sad news" to which I replied, "Nonsense. Sure, maybe this team is not what your Father has in mind, but He is going to keep blessing your socks off. Never look to anyone, no team, no one, only your Father. The blessings **will** come *through* Him, just keep saying that, and be excited—live expectantly."

The viper had jumped out of another fire, grabbed hold of my son, but thank You, Darling, when I spoke the truth in faith, he agreed with me, which shook that serpent and the curse off his livelihood. It was less than an hour later when I heard my son cheering loudly downstairs! He had a message on his phone saying that he had a week's worth of work, on a brand-new job that would pay him five times more than he's ever been paid!!

This is still wordy what do you think?

Oh, joy!! Our Husband, our children's Father, asks us this question each time someone tells us of the impossibilities coming against us. He says, "Behold, I am the LORD, the God of all flesh; is anything too difficult for Me?" (Jeremiah 32:27). My son and I answered Him, expressing our love by our responses, which said, "Ah Lord GOD! Behold, You have made the heavens and the earth by Your great power and by Your outstretched arm! NOTHING is too difficult for You"! (Jeremiah 32:17).

Another testimony I'd like to share concerns my sister who has an awesome testimony that I believe will bless many of you who are concerned about your excess weight and health issues. Though this book focuses primarily on our finances, the poverty mentality can spread over your entire life: touching every area (it can take hold of such as) including your health. And the greater the blessing, the stronger the viper will try to take hold of you and your miracles.

My sister, bless her heart, is well past retirement age—however, she is physically able to function as a young teenager, but emotionally she functions at the age of little girl. Much like Erin's sister, Aunt Patty Cake, my sister has been a blessing, even though this has been a hard life for her. What I find that's so wonderful is that my sister, and so many like her, have the faith of a child. I love being around that. Unlike most of us, my sister doesn't lack a heavenly Husband, but instead needs a Father (since our father passed away), so like my children, this is Who I've encouraged her to look to for her needs.

Due to her age, my sister has begun to suffer from many ailments, so all of us have encouraged her to go up for prayer each week and to keep submitting prayer request, but mostly to keep believing that God can heal her—rather than running to her doctor. It was almost a month ago when she called me with the exciting news. She had documentation from her doctor that God had healed her from high blood pressure AND from diabetes!!

My sister had noticed that her blood sugar stayed the same each time that she checked it—even after she cheated! Just like a little child who breaks the rules, so does my sister. I'd caught her several times when she stayed with me eating all sorts of candy, but even in her naughtiness her Father used it for good to show her how He had healed her!! No one could believe it. It got her much attention throughout the church family that she happily basked in for weeks! Just like a child, she would tell everyone she met how GOD had healed her of high blood pressure and diabetes.

Next she told me that she wanted to lose weight and she was very bold to tell me *God* would help her lose the weight. I had told her months earlier that she shouldn't try to *do* anything, but instead to just keep trusting and believing that *God* would do it, showing her the verse in the Bible that she marked and read out loud at every meal. "So don't worry about these things, saying, 'What will we eat? What will we drink? What will we wear?" These things dominate the thoughts of unbelievers, but your heavenly Father already knows all your needs." (Matthew 6:3)

It was only a few weeks later my sister called to tell me that the director of her group had contacted her doctor hoping he would prescribe something for her to get rid of her recent nausea. She told me that she never felt like eating and if she did, she could only eat very little before feeling nauseous, and her caretakers were worried about her.

Excitedly I told her that this may be His plan to give her the desires of her heart, to be thin again, and not to try to stop what He might have chosen for "His diet plan" for her. I told her that He accomplishes His plan in different ways, but I felt sure it was God, and to simply not take any more medicine.

Almost daily my sister would call excitedly to tell me she was in a smaller size, and then the viper struck! I got a call from the director of her group home who was very angry and told me my sister was trying to "starve herself." She told me she refused to eat and how unhealthy it was to do it that way.

Thankfully, I decided to be as bold as my sister, but lovingly told her that this was not the truth. That my sister was not "trying to starve herself" but that in fact she was trusting God to lose the weight she had put on after moving to her group home. That her lack of appetite (the nausea was no longer there) was a blessing she had trusted God for, and that my sister told me that she only ate when she was hungry, chose better food than the junk she was eating and felt great!

Nevertheless the viper just wouldn't let go, as the director continued yelling at me that it was simply not healthy to lose weight that fast, to which I voiced the truth. I lovingly said that that being overweight was also not healthy, and the speed of her weight loss was all God's doing. She went on to tell me that "God's plan for losing weight" was in a book she had given my sister, and that this is how my sister needed to go about properly losing her weight. With a final shake, I told her that God's plan is to *simply* trust Him.

Not only did my sister lose all the weight that she'd hope to lose, but God blessed her with a new dress to wear to her nephew's wedding. When she first got it she said she couldn't zip it up, so I told her I would find her something else to wear, but God stopped me with a reminder of my past. Years earlier I had gotten a pair of pajamas that I could not even pull up past my knees because they were so tight, but when I went to return them, I heard my Husband say I shouldn't. That's when, inside my spirit, it hit me that He was telling me I would be thin again! So I told her my testimony and said that she should do the same thing—to just hang the dress out where she could see it and each time thank her Father for when it would fit. Within a couple of weeks she called to say, "My dress fits and I look beautiful!!"

Dear bride, whether the viper is holding on to you regarding your health, weight, finances, or a relationship, shake it off. Speak the word of truth, in faith due to your love for Him, and watch your miracle appear!

In the book of Revelation God tells us that we will overcome the wicked one by His blood and by the *word* of each other's testimonies. Let me then end this chapter with another testimony of my own.

My Eleventh of Many Financial Testimonies

"Believing for Big Things"

It's on the eve of this chapter being posted on the Encouraging Women website that I just had to share with you a testimony follow up and to say that *none of us* has any idea just how our Husband *longs* to bless us when we simply believe Him for bigger things as it says in Ephesians 3:20 TLB, "Now glory be to God, who by his mighty power at work within us is able to do far more than we would ever dare to ask or even dream of—infinitely beyond our highest prayers, desires, thoughts, or hopes."

Funny how it is not until we turn to Him, often due to some sort of struggle we have, that brings us to the place of speaking to Him about those bigger, grander desires. Can you relate?

The vacation I shared about in the last chapter got a bit longer due to feeling just a bit more exhausted than vacations usually make us. Getting too little sleep on the last night of our stay convinced me that what I sensed He was telling me to do was to drive only half way home. However, I was in a difficult position since I hadn't brought any maps with me (and this was before you could just pull up a map on your phone)— so I wasn't sure just where the halfway point was! Later I reflected that *not* bringing my maps was part of His plan too.

While still in my room, the Lord led me to book a hotel online in a city I wasn't sure was even on my way home. Booking online at the last minute is no big deal; it was doing it without seeing a map that made the task of booking a room just about impossible for me.

May I say that my Husband is doing a new thing in my life, to encourage me to live even more abundantly, by having Him lead me (for the most part) blindfolded through some impossible tasks?

My first blindfolded impossible task began when I did my taxes just last week—taxes are something that is personally impossible for me to do. Rewinding, our taxes have always been difficult, due mainly to our complicated situation and were a feat that my ex-husband never attempted and he was good at things like that, so he always turned them over to the professionals. Yet, here I was, me, the "fool" doing them—and in just one day—even though they have proved challenging for professionals who'd taken weeks to do them— blindfolded (since I had no clue what I was doing) got them done!

The day after I mailed my taxes I know that my Husband was up to something, because not only are these feats a way to encourage others, He will also use them to help bring us to a place of remembering those feats to help us to do more with Him. Just a week later, He reminded me of doing my taxes blindfolded, something that was simply impossible for me to do, when He led me to book a hotel blindfolded without knowing where it was.

As I drove, and the closer I got to our halfway point, I had to force myself not to think too much and not to worry. The reason is simply, whenever you or I are stressed or concerned, we cannot hear Him well enough, which means we often hear Him incorrectly. I'd say it's sort of like spiritual interference because His communication is blocked by our fear. Maybe that is why there are 365 times that God tells us *not* to fear in the Bible.

Even though what He had me do initially was incredible, it was the turn of events that got my attention, and has done so much to help me see just how our Husband wants to bless us—if we simply let go and fully trust Him and tune into His leading us, blindfolded.

Just a few minutes before we were about to arrive at our hotel, the one I booked online, my daughter said she needed to stop to use the restroom. So I immediately pulled off the highway at the very next exit. As I turned off I saw a gas station on the first corner, but I could sense He was leading me to go to another station down the street. And as I drove, I noticed the name of the hotel directly across the street: it was the name of the chain I'd booked online (a hotel chain I was not familiar with). Rather than be excited, fear tried to grip me because it looked a bit seedy [seedy is defined as shabby, dirty-looking, and often disreputable] and certainly not a place I wanted to bring my children.

My fear was not that we would be harmed, but the fear was that I had missed hearing Him correctly. I know that ALL of you can relate. I just wanted to share this with you because I believe that many of you wonder if people like me are ever concerned. The answer is yes; I believe everyone experiences flashes of concern and doubt—especially when we move forward boldly. The enemy will always put those kinds of thoughts in your head, but it's what you do with these thoughts and fears that will make the ultimate difference in your life for the better or worse.

Immediately when fear tried to reign, I began to simply speak to Him and ask Him to help me to know what to do next. Within two minutes I was walking out of the gas station and noticed one of those throw away magazines that said "coupons" on it. Let me tell you that I always ignore these. Always. But today He led me to pick it up and then without thinking, I simply handed it to my daughter in the back seat of the car.

Again without really thinking (just as He led me to do while doing my taxes) I asked her to look in the magazine for the city where the other hotel was located. As this was happening I sensed how He was leading me step-by-step. She said there were four hotels listed, but since there was traffic, I couldn't fully listen, which I realize is also part of His plan for me not to think, but to be led by Him.

As I got off the highway on our exit, I could sense the Lord leading me to go to the hotel I had booked, look at it, and then I would know. It took only a tiny peek in the window of one of the rooms for the confirmation that this was **not** where He wanted us to stay. Turning around, I told the children that after booking He'd also led me to look at the fine print (another thing I never did) saying that I could cancel and not be charged for the room *if* I canceled before 6 P.M.; it was 5:10. So immediately I pulled over, and called to cancel the reservation.

Exhausted, I asked Him (out loud) to lead me, and pulled into a driveway a half a block down the road, not even knowing what the hotel was, but it looked nice as we drove closer. Then the children noticed an indoor pool and Jacuzzi and began to cheer, so I went inside the lobby.

It was just as I was closing the car door that the Lord prompted me to bring the coupon book that my daughter was holding and I asked her while we walked in if this hotel was in the book. The funny thing is, neither of us noticed the name of the hotel we were walking in to it, yet the minute I stepped up to the desk the lady saw the book in my hand and said, "You know, that book has the most amazing deal in it" and promptly took the book from my hand, cut out the coupon, and asked me if I wanted a room by the pool!

Honestly, I felt like I was in some sort of a dream; I was so tired and couldn't make sense of what was happening. She told me the room included a delicious all-you-can-eat breakfast (not the continental coffee and donuts that most offer), and when we got to our room we found not just a room—but a huge expansive suite!! The cost?? It was almost *half the cost* of the seedy hotel that I had booked, then canceled, online!

Dear bride, it takes just one thing to make miracles happen in our lives—it is simply believing our Husband for big things—allowing ourselves to be led by Him! Let go, stop thinking, and take His hand was He leads you to your next miracle!!

─────────── Chapter 12 ───────────

Who Said?

"So faith comes from hearing,
and hearing by the word of God."
—Romans 10:17

This week I purchased three copies of *Supernatural Childbirth* for three weddings that are taking place this year: my two sons and also a dear friend, who, by the way, is in her mid-thirties. She never believed she would marry, but not only is marrying, but her husband wants children right away! Isn't that so God?

Yet, as the set of books sat there I couldn't help but want to share them with my daughters, so that when they see all the women screaming on television shows or in movies they will be able to dispel the fears that birth is both painful and dangerous, since "faith comes from hearing, and hearing by the word of God" (Romans 10:17). Instead, as believers, He said we have been set free from curses and sins.

So I began reading from the book to my daughters, but it wasn't until I had begun interjecting my own faith as we read that I realized God had led me to share this truth about childbirth for the same reason that we taught our children about Creationism—so that they could snicker (rather than agree) when they heard "billions and billions of years ago"—knowing the truth regarding the age of the earth is closer to just 7,000 years.

In this final chapter, I want to focus on just one thing, Who Said? Who said was the response that the author of *Supernatural Childbirth* heard from her future husband. Who Said? is something I believe we all should ask ourselves—especially anytime we, or someone else, tries to limit our lives with why we can't do something or why something can't be done (like trusting God with our debt).

"Who said?" was the question Jackie Maze's fiancé asked just after she had told him that she couldn't have children. Rather than accept this as fact, his response was, "Who said?" And as he went on to say, and the book goes on to say, this question really matters since most of what we say, and what others say, is NOT what God says (about us or our situation). When Jackie and her husband married they chose to believe what GOD said and as a result had four children—along with supernatural, pain-free births!

So when people *say* that single moms like me, raising four children alone, means struggles and difficulties that will adversely affect my children's stability and future. And even though these were dear friends, Christians, who asked, expressing the sentiments with gloom in their voices. Each was surprised that my children always respond gleefully when asked "How IS your family doing?" they answer "Great!" with big smiles.

Most have only heard the rumors, so I can only imagine if they knew the details (like no child support, and having our resource warehouse emptied out and stolen by my ex-husband). Because I'm sure they would be more than just a little surprised—they'd be shocked wondering how we could possibly be doing "Great!" That's only because, like the world, most Christians believe what they *see*. And what they typically *see* are Christians who live in despair and lack just like the world does. They believe, as the world does, that it takes a husband, two incomes, earning or working hard to make it—not *simply* because of God's promise that He **says** He will supply all of our needs when we trust Him to do so.

So let me ask you:

Who said you don't have enough to pay your bills?

Who said you can't afford that new dress, to eat out, to take a vacation?

Unfortunately, oftentimes it's *we* who are the ones making these negative statements never realizing that what we say, therefore, will become our reality.

When it's someone else who is speaking this way about us, then it's time to stop discussing our present situation with people, even Christians, who don't believe God's Word. Remember, faith comes by hearing, and if you are not speaking, then you'll be listening and hearing the Word of God spoken about your situation. You will no longer find that His promises and abundance are eluding your life. So often it is when I hear myself say something negative that it pierces my spirit: I almost can feel it take hold of my heart.

The reason our words have such power because it says He lives within each one of us, as believers. This means, we, too, have the power to speak powerful effects into existence in the same way God created the world, and the way Jesus calmed the storms, or broke a few loaves of bread to feed thousands. Do you remember what the disciples said about feeding the masses, not once but twice, saying that there wouldn't be enough? But **God** *said* He would supply.

So, the question must always be, "Who said?"

Isn't it time that you and I choose to break free from the poverty mentality and prove the greatness of God?

There is a world of desperate people out there that are full of needs, and we are the ones who hold the keys to their hope.

To change the world, it will take us believing to the point that we *live* in the fact that God **will** provide for *all* our needs. It does not say that

He *might* supply *some* of our needs, does it? As a matter of fact, it doesn't seem to have a condition to this promise at all—it simply says, that He *will* supply. *True, the enemy does have permission to come and steal, so be sure you keep what He gives by your tithes and offerings.

Just recently I have found that my greatest desire is to have everything that Jesus, my Husband (and yours), died to give me, and in turn, teach this truth to as many people as I can. Most believe only that Jesus died in order to make it into heaven. Yet, it's much more than what happens when we die! What He left us is so much more that only a very few ever realize. It's not about what happens when we die, but how He wants us to live—live as His bride—and live this life abundantly!!

Trying to explain this to my younger children, I told them it is much like people with a new cell phone. Some, like my sister who's in a group home, can place a call and get one; unfortunately, for her to see if someone called her, or if someone left a message, is beyond her capacity to understand. Nevertheless, the cell phone she has does many more things that she could benefit from *if* she knew how to use it. Then there are my children who can do more on a cell phone than I can, and I believe this will be true for their Christian journey as well.

Our Husband can do much more for our lives than a new cell phone, but so few are willing to break away from the way they have always believed, by simply listening, learning and thus believing Him for more. To help our children, loved ones and women in this world, you and I must **break free from the poverty mentality** that speaks and believes in a life of lack. No, not so we can boast, brag, or flaunt what we have. Instead, we are simply to let our light, our lives, shine so that others know that our Beloved, lived and died in order to set us free from not having enough—to live a life of abundance.

This has become my one passion.

Personally, I don't want one drop of His precious blood to be shed in vain, but to be used to prove that He not only exists, but He *longs* to love and cherish each of the lost who have yet to meet Him personally. To gather together all the brides who long to be loved and taken care of so they, too, can be caught up into His loving arms and embraced the way I am each and every day.

As we have learned throughout this book, the poverty mentality is not just about money, instead, it is breaking free from the bondage of lack. Being rid of the fear of *lack* of money will set us all free from *lack* in every area of our lives—due to fully understanding and experiencing His love.

Either HE is all we need or He isn't.

I say He is more than we could ever need or want—therefore, my life must reflect this belief for me to break free from the poverty mentality and learn to move mountains. Want to come along?

My Twelfth and final of Many Financial Testimonies

"By Your Words"

Once again, as I mentioned with the last chapter's testimony, I had so many testimonies to choose from for this final chapter. My dilemma was which one should I share with you? So, as I began discussing this problem with my Husband, then waited for Him to show me, He, instead, gave me a NEW and extremely exciting testimony. Something wonderful that blessed me and what I believe will bless you too!

It was almost a year ago, during Spring, that I began landscaping our home. When my ex and I moved it, it was a new home which had never been lived it, and therefore, only had sparse grass around it. What my Husband began to do was incredible as it began to unfold. Without having a plan, He began to lead me to find a few small plants, a small tree, and some decorative rocks so my sons and I could landscape our home just like you'd see in a magazine. Each time I'd look outside or drive up to our home, my heart felt like it could burst, it went way beyond the desires of my heart. As amazing as this was, He was not done.

Our backyard is what everyone sees first since we were on a corner, and our builder had said it still needed a lower deck built. So, because he told us that when we purchased the home, I also thought it's what was needed to finish it. Yet, that's not what He said. Since my ex left, and I became His bride, I have discovered that my Husband is also interested in decorating our home and that He has things for us that are way beyond what we could hope or imagine ourselves. All He asks is that we simply fall in love with Him, because He longs, yes, *longs,* to bless us as His bride far beyond our wildest dreams!

It didn't take long for my Darling to show me that a deck was not His plan for our home, so I refocused and found a young man that went to my son's church who specialized in patios. Basically, using stone rather than wood as the foundation. It was all set for him to get started while I was away in South America, Africa, and Europe, but then just before I left he got a huge client and he had to reschedule my job for later in September when I would be returning home.

Yet when I returned home, I had no money. It wasn't the cost of the trip, which had been paid for by a dear friend more than a year earlier… didn't I tell you that God would provide for *all* your needs and whatever He calls you too? I'm not sure what caused the funds to not be there, nor did I ponder for long. I knew that it's by not having money for something that God redirects us and teaches us new things. He'll use this to unfold His plan for our future. That's why we should never, ever panic or listen to the lie that says we don't have enough due to Him not supplying our needs. Waiting for what we hope for never means no. Instead, it means that He has something even better waiting for us when we simply rejoice and trust Him.

Do you remember the testimony of the ring in chapter 6? It was during this same draught, "For he will be like a tree planted by the water, that extends its roots by a stream and will not fear when the heat comes; but its leaves will be green, and it will not be anxious in a **year** of drought nor cease to yield **fruit**" (Jeremiah 17:8), when, **if** I had had the money to pay for the patio stone (or the ring) back then in September, things would have turned out much differently, and, there also would have been no testimony to share with anyone. Isn't this what our life is all about?

Our lives are to be living testimonies of how His abundant bride lives—in order that the world will know—just how wonderful He *really, truly* is. This is what will ultimately cause most to open their hearts to Him and His love too! Yet, for this to happen, people must see our trust in Him, showing others that He will go way beyond just providing for our needs, but instead, our Bridegroom *longs* to give us the desires of our hearts when we simply trust that He will.

When I didn't have the money for the patio, I called the young man who more than understood my desire to wait to see what the Lord wanted to do. Fall led to winter, then spring arrived again, when I sensed that my wait was just about over, so I started to speak to Him about it once again. Waiting, then sensing it was time to speak to Him about it, led to me seeing a much grander picture when one day I spotted an outdoor living room set at my local membership warehouse. It was a gorgeous shade of red that took my breath away. So I grabbed a brochure with a picture, took it home, so I could look at it regularly and to ask my Husband for it.

If you read my book, *Facing Divorce Again*, you may remember in Chapter 11 "The Danger of a Poverty Mentality" that it took me asking for my front load washer and dryer for my Husband to give me something that each and every single day I think about and thank Him for—and a testimony I share with everyone I meet!

However, due to my older son's concern about the amount of our rising debt, which our family now owes, I've spoken to my Husband about it every chance I get—mainly due to the magnitude and enormity of this ever-rising crisis. Though I can't elaborate on it now, I promise that by the end of my next book *Moving Mountains*, you should be able to understand fully the amount of debt that He has promised HE will throw into the sea, which will happen by faith and understanding the scope of His love. This is how I know it will happen.

Dear bride, will you join me in believing it too, for your situation? Rather than haphazardly throwing our faith around helter-skelter, we must be careful to believe what He says, not what we want Him to say. And the reason is simple—because misguided and false faith, believing what we want rather than what He's truth revealed to us, damages the faith of all those who are watching. Okay, now let me get back to my testimony when we were talking about the outdoor living room for the patio I didn't have money to pay for.

After looking at the furniture, speaking to my Husband about it, the furniture ended up being paid for by my tax refund—which covered the entire cost! But the testimony wasn't getting a tax refund. What got my children's attention was that this was the first time that I filed taxes!! Remember the last chapter's testimony, when I said that our taxes, due to our complicated situation, were a feat that my ex-husband never attempted to do and he was good at things like that? Everyone told us that our taxes had to be done professionally since they are far too complicated than most. Just pulling all the information for the accountant took my ex-husband three months—months, that my children remembered him yelling and was so angry throughout the process due to the stress.

Yet, when the taxes were left to me, my Husband told me that He would guide me to do them myself. My children watched as their new Father, my Husband, guided me step-by-step—finishing in less than 8 hours!! I didn't even take off homeschooling my children. Instead, their Father told me to simply homeschool two *half* days, and when I was done, in the afternoon, He and I did the taxes together. Not only was it not stressful—it was a wonderful time where we became closer—when I could fully feel His love for me.

May I say too, like so many things, to gain the spiritual strength to do them, He told me to wait, because as we should know that's it's those who "wait upon the LORD shall renew their strength; they shall mount up with wings as eagles; they shall run, and not be weary; and they shall walk, and not faint." Isaiah 40:31. So I waited, and waited, then with only two days left, I started, then finished on the day my taxes were due. Even now I am in complete utter awe at what transpired!

Okay, once again, let me get back to my testimony. Our patio began to unfold on a Friday when I sensed He was showing me to go and rotate my car's tires at the discount warehouse where I'd seen the outdoor furniture. Since they said the wait would be more than an hour, I told my children and my sister (who was with us) that we should go sit on that furniture "we were getting" so we could enjoy our time while getting excited again about whatever it was that He was going to do. (This was before my tax return, which by the way, never once has our family ever gotten a tax return.)

Just minutes after we sat down, a friend whom I hadn't seen for more than four years came walking up. She sat with us and my joy began to spill over. I told her so many things the Lord, my new Husband, had been doing for our family. That's when I mentioned about the furniture that we were sitting in, that I sensed we would be getting as soon as we knew how my children's new Father wanted us to create our patio. That's when she told me that her husband, a contractor, was close friends with the best concrete man in the area and he'd be happy come over to help us!!

Though everyone was excited, I knew the cost would surely be high. (The truth is, I still have a bank account that is filled due to the car I never bought for my daughter. Money, I am still waiting to see what my Husband wants me to do with it. And as I said in a previous chapter, I do have an insurmountable amount of debt to pay off, but unless my Husband shows me what to do, I simply wait.) Once again, knowing my older boys' concerns, I could sense that their Father had a plan that was beginning to unfold.

The very next morning, a Saturday, the only day of the week to sleep in, I woke up just after 4 A.M. wide awake with a tremendous urge to go to the post office, envisioning opening my post office box. However, I told myself (I didn't say this to my Husband, though I know He was next to me listening to my thoughts), that I didn't *want* to go to the post office, how crazy I was to think such a thing, and to just go back to sleep! That's when I heard my daughter's new puppy being taken outside, once again, so I got up and took her for my daughter so she could sleep in. Notice how gently our Husband will nudge us when it's something He doesn't want us to miss?

Once up, I decided I would beat the crowds and go shopping (taking the puppy with me of course). The night before while lying in bed, I remembered that when we take just a tiny step in the right direction of obedience to the Lord's promptings, our miracle will suddenly appear. Remember, it was when Joshua took that first step into the Jordan River that it parted? So as I drove, like always, I began talking to my Husband. "In all your ways *acknowledge* Him [He's sitting right there beside you so why ignore Him?], and He will make your paths straight [saving you so much time having to figure it out]" (Proverbs 3:6). That morning He led me to go get the rock for the flowerbeds, and that was my first step in my Jordan.

Just as I was heading straight for the rock quarry by our home, I made a quick right turn and headed to the post office. When I got there I began opening letters one-by-one. When I came to the last one I stood there reading the note enclosed first, and then, I looked at the amount of the check that was from a dear friend who said she'd been blessed and her Husband told her to send me half "as a thank you for me introducing her to her Husband." The check was made out for thousands of dollars—*more* than enough to pay for my patio and so much more!! I was so excited it felt that my heart would burst!

Though I wanted to rush home and wake everyone, my Husband wanted to be alone with me for a bit longer, so we continued to the quarry so I could purchase the rock, and then I headed home to share the awesome news with my children who were already awake when I returned.

When we sat down to eat breakfast, that's when I told them what had happened that morning, from not wanting to get up, to being nudged by hearing my daughter taking out the puppy. Each and every detail was part of God's plan, their Father's plan, even us having breakfast! It had been months since we were able to all eat Saturday breakfast together so I'd mentioned it to their Father the prior week.

After our big breakfast, we all went outside on our patio wooden deck just off the kitchen, which a few weeks later became the ceiling for the outdoor living space. Since then we've spent many afternoons talking in that space, and evenings roasting marshmallows over the fire pit. Almost always our conversations begin by talking about how that special space came to be and about the new Husband and Father we've been blessed to have!

Darling reader, please always remember this, our Husband has a plan and will build each of our testimonies. To do so, He very often will withhold funds at times to redirect us and ask us to wait while He creates those miracles, which happen in His perfect timing. He may use a puppy or something else, like a rude phone call, to wake us up if we are determined to sleep in, and finish by gathering those we love when the testimony is ready to be shared!

Never underestimate His love for us, since it is our faith, hope, and trust in our Husband that unleashes the miracles that He longs to do every day in our lives! Live with great expectations and you, too, will break free of the poverty mentality and begin to *Move Mountains!*

About the Author

Michele Michaels came to Restore Ministries International when she was facing divorce. At the time she was the mother of two small boys. After reading *How God Can and Will Restore Your Marriage* and *A Wise Woman* and she began helping Erin Thiele with her books, soon after they met while each were in Orlando, Florida. Very soon after Erin visited Michele in her home in Colorado, her marriage was restored.

Almost exactly fourteen years later Michele found herself facing divorce again while helping to update and revise a small Facing Divorce booklet for her church. After returning to RMI to Refresh her mind, Michele began to realize He had planned to use this trial for much good. It was during this new chapter in her life when Michele discovered the real reason God allowed another divorce to happen again and what she had been missing: The Abundant Life.

Look for Michele's next books on Encouraging Bookstore.com and also on Amazon.com: *Finding the Abundant Life, Living the Abundant Life* and *Moving Mountains* to watch how her Abundant Life unfolds as she travels with her Heavenly Husband along her Restoration Journey.

Check what is Also Available
on EncouragingBookstore.com & Amazon.com

Scan the code below to the available books for our Abundant Life, Restored and By the Word of Their Testimony series.

Please visit our Websites where you'll also find these books as FREE Courses for both men and women.

Want to know more how you can Live an Abundant Life?

Restore Ministries International
POB 830 Ozark, MO 65721

For more help
Please visit one of our Websites:

EncouragingWomen.org

HopeAtLast.com

LoveAtLast.org

RestoreMinistries.net

RMIEW.com

RMIOU.com

Aidemaritale.com (French)

AjudaMatrimonial.com (Portuguese)

AmoreSenzaFine.com (Italian)

AyudaMatrimonial.com (Spanish)

Eeuwigdurendeliefde-nl.com (Dutch)

EternalLove-jp.com (Japanese)

EvliliginiKurtar.com (Turkish)

Pag-asa.org (Tagalog Filipino)

UiteindelikHoop.com (Afrikaans)

Wiecznamilosc.com (Polish)

ZachranaManzelstva.com (Slovak)

EncouragingMen.org

www.ingramcontent.com/pod-product-compliance
Lightning Source LLC
La Vergne TN
LVHW021354080426
835508LV00020B/2279